George Condon

Gaels of Laughter and Tears

All About Interesting Irish Characters
from Cleveland (Little Achill)
& Other Byways ,
With Special Reference
to the Nickname Game

By George E. Condon

Illustrated by Richard (Doodles) Dugan

Published by Waterford Books
P.O. Box 770394
Cleveland, Ohio 44107

Library of Congress Catalog Card Number

ISBN 0-9649268-0-6

Printed in the United States of America

Contents

Old Friends Remembered   1

Getting a Nickname the Hard Way   20

The Waiting Game   22

On the Dilemma of a Horn   23

Holy Water Mike   24

The Day the Cookie Crumbled   28

The Day Steve Brodie became the Fall Guy   32

When Bullets Lost the War   37

His Whispers Caught Their Ears   38

Nicknames of the Cleveland Irish   39

Now It Can Be Told   54

Clothes Make the Boy-o   67

In the Line of Duty   68

A Little goes a Long Way   70

The Miracle of Television   71

Hitting the Bottle to Advantage   73

With a Song on His Lips   74

Sergt. Muldoon at Valley Forge   82

Mulraney and the Milkman   84

Hark, the Herald's a Boy!   87

Dominus Vobiscum   88

The Power of Speech   91

Donuts Had a Word for It   92

The Parade that almost Wasn't   94

Freckles & His Friends   97

The Cowboy at Large   98

The Case of the Sleepy Bailiff   100

The Road to Ruane   103

The Battler from Linndale   104

Down-to-Earth Wisdom   114

Skid Strikes Back   116

Dedication

This book is dedicated to Kelly Anne Love, Peter George Brereton, and Patrick Condon Brereton—with love from Grandpa.

In Appreciation

Many friendly hands helped in this work, but special thanks are owed to Dr. William (Bill) McKinley Randle, Thomas F. Stanton, Neil McReynolds, William Spellacy, Gerard Souza, Jeffrey Leitch, Donna Conway, Tom Kelly, Raymond (Rip) Reilly, Don Kelly, John Coyne, Tom O'Connell, Brian Hodgkinson, Linn Sheldon, Al Sutton, Bernie Toorish, and my brothers, John Condon and Maurice Condon.

BOOKS BY GEORGE E. CONDON

Gaels of Laughter and Tears
The Man in the Arena: The Al Sutphin Story
Cleveland: The Best-Kept Secret
Laughter from the Rafters
Stars in the Water: The Story of the Erie Canal
Yesterday's Cleveland
Yesterday's Columbus
Cleveland: Prodigy of the Western Reserve
History of the Ohio Farmers Insurance Company

Old Friends Remembered

There can be no true telling of the West Side story in Cleveland that does not take loving notice of the names of so many of its people. Not necessarily the surnames like the Murphys, O'Briens, Sweeneys, Corrigans, Butlers, Sullivans, O'Reillys, Mastersons, O'Malleys and all the rest of the Hibernian aristocracy, mind you. They have been given all the notice and respect they can handle without losing their heads entirely.

The matter of nicknames is something else again. They and their bearers long ago were relegated to the lowbrow level by social arbiters who could not stand such irreverence and lack of formality. It's a rather serious misunderstanding that ought to be set aright before it's too late. A nickname is nothing to trifle with.

Many hundreds of nicknames grew to full flower through the years in the garden of immigrants that flourished in the City of Ohio and its successor neighborhoods within Cleveland, especially on the near West Side.

It is true that nicknames were to be found among all the nationalities that settled there, to be sure, but more commonly in the Irish community than the others. Even the mother of the famous Cleveland composer, Ernest Roland Ball, had a nickname. She was "Mother Machree," and it was Ball who wrote the Irish ballad in her honor.

The substitution of sobriquets for baptismal names flourished most noticeably when the Irish population of the near West Side was at its highest, which also was the time when the interrelationship of the people was at its closest. The sense of loneliness that made them huddle together in a foreign land was the very thing that brought them together in the kind of segregation that lent comfort.

It followed inevitably that when so many people of the same ethnic background lived closely together, there would be widespread duplication of family names. That presented no problem to the young people. They simply skirted around duplications by giving each other fresh identities that they considered more appropriate, thus separating each individual from all the rest.

It wasn't only among young people that nicknames flourished. Adults often shared in the practice, as they still do, by hanging pet names on their children, not always to his or her advantage. It is all very well for a five-year-old to be known at home and among friends as "Buddy," or "Sonny," but the same name carried to adulthood may be a liability. There aren't many bank presidents named "Sonny."

While nicknames flourished as a kind of living art form when a lot of Irish lived closely together in the pioneer neighborhoods, the custom lost strength as the homogenous population was diluted by the infusion of other nationalities. Nicknames apparently represented an outgrowth of the intimate, informal relationship that best thrives, perhaps, among people of common background and temperament. The element of informality, which is the very essence of the practice, is less likely to be found in ethnic mixtures.

The popularity and proliferation of nicknames among the West Side Irish and their descendants, incidentally, is not peculiar to Cleveland by any means. The sobriquets that this city offers in such abundance are to be found in similar immigrant colonies of Irish in other American cities. Young Ronald Reagan, born in Tampico, Illinois, far from the mainstream of Irish settlement, acquired the nickname of "Dutch." A sense of humor, after all, knows no political boundaries; it follows the race.

A prominent example of the universality of nicknames among the Irish is to be found in Boston, as one would expect, because it has probably the largest Celtic colony in America. Irish nicknames, most of them improbable, flourished there more abundantly than in any other city. A leading example was President John F. Kennedy's grandfather, the longtime mayor of Boston, John Fitzgerald, best known as Honey Fitzgerald.

Among Boston's most famous sons in recent decades was the Speaker of the U. S. House of Representatives, Thomas P. O'Neill, whose baptismal name was almost unknown. The nation joined his old chums back home in referring to him simply as Tip O'Neill.

Tip O'Neill grew up in a North Cambridge neighborhood whose residents were not to be confused with the Harvard crowd in that other Cambridge neighborhood. He and his friends from childhood gathered informally at a favorite place they called Barry's Corner, whose focus point was the stoop in front of the home of the Barry brothers on Rindge Avenue. Among the regulars in that group were none other than Pinky Sullivan, Skippy McCaffrey, Mickey O'Neil, Redfish Fitzgerald, Potatoes Labo, Blubber Sheehan, and Hambone Sullivan.

It was said that an uncle gave Tip his nickname in recollection of another Tip O'Neill, an old-time baseball player who was notorious for his ability to foul-tip pitch after pitch until he drew a walk from the weary pitcher. The latter-day O'Neill wore down his political adversaries in much the same way. But he who carried a nickname through his long lifetime also was creative in giving novel new identities to others among his friends.

For example, Pinky Sullivan, formally named James, got his new name when a girl, passing the group of young men sitting on Barry's front steps, said, "Hi, Jimmy." Tip O'Neill turned to the bashful Sullivan and observed, "You're pink!" From that day on, he was Pinky to one and all. In such a spontaneous way were nicknames born in Boston, as in Cleveland. They were usually creditable appellations, accepted as a sign of recognition and comradely affection.

*   *   *

In the beginning, when life was simpler, so were the names.

The heritage of the centuries is wrapped in names, but the cognominal system developed slowly and simply, arising gradually in response to need, not plan, as do almost all human advances.

Nicknames undoubtedly formed the first level in the many-tiered development of the name system. It isn't likely that anybody came into the world during cave man days bearing the name of, say, Quentin Thistlewaite III.

Physical characteristics led to names, as did occupations, places of origin, ancestry and personal traits. All went into the name barrel in the first crude days of name-dropping and remain there to this day. But the steady increase in population brought on a new complexity by doubling a person's nickname; that is, by adding surnames to the given name. A child born with russet locks immediately was given the name of "Red." But there were a lot of redheads, so if the kid's father was named John, he became known as Red, John's son. It was an easy bridge to Red Johnson. Two nicknames for the price of one.

A nickname has the same reinforcing effect in building an identity as the flying buttress does in architecture. It tends to give recognition, where the surname does not, to certain physical, mental, or moral characteristics of the person in question. A nickname in fact is a revealing capsule, a compressed description, and, sometimes, the ultimate brevity in the use of satire, sarcasm, affection, or truth itself. It could even be the most successful example of the art of the short story.

In the medieval past, interestingly enough, it was not uncommon to amplify a name with a personal description. The history books are full of references to such notables as Pepin the Short, Louis the Pious, and Charles the Bald. It was a sensible way to single out some persons and is still used in some quarters, especially in the neighborhood pool parlor, where references to regulars like Looey the Louse, Herman the Fink, and Eddy the Chump can be heard at any time.

Proper people who disapprove of nicknames will shudder at such a crude practice. They see sobriquets of that kind as lowbrow and vulgar, not appreciating that names of all kinds ought to be appreciated for their originality and dynamic quality.

As the identification system expanded to keep pace with a growing population, names became linked with occupations, leading any number of coopers, carpenters, thatchers, masons, tailors, farmers and porters to make a name for themselves—among them such notables as Margaret Thatcher, James Mason, Eddie Cantor and Red Barber.

As world numbers rise, the name field, like the universe itself, is ever expanding. Meeting the challenge is not always easy or successful. At last count, the world had 75,000,000 (million) persons named Chang. The Chinese need of nicknames has to be desperate.

The creative way that American parents have rallied around to meet the name problem is to be admired. The originality of their family names constitutes a special field of study whose leading authority is Author John Train, who recalls in (*Most Remarkable Names, 1977. Clarkson N. Potter, Inc., Publishers, New York*) that a child was given the name of Nosmo King because its mother, wondering what to call her newborn, drew inspiration from a sign in the hospital corridor: No Smoking.

The child is joined on Train's honor roll of names by hundreds of standouts, such as Immaculate Conception Finkelstein, Positive Wasserman Johnson, Katz Meow, and Faux Pas Bidet.

It may be that nobody appreciated the importance and influence of names more than Charles Dickens. They were a conspicuous part of his literary contribution. No writer ever matched Dickens as a coiner of names so openly calculated to advance his stories through their subliminal effect on the minds of readers. No plot or literary ornamentation is needed to support such outstanding names as Ebenezer Scrooge, Mr. Pickwick, Martin Chuzzlewit, Mr. Gradgrind, Sir Mulberry Hawk, Uriah Heep, Mr. Pecksniff, Oliver Twist, Serjeant Buzfus, Canon Crisparkle, Susan Nipper, Mr. Guppy, Lord Coodle and Sir Thomas Doodle.

With such names, Dickens carried the nomenclature of his creative works to a level never approached by other writers. They are nicknames that ring with onomatopoeiac effect, yielding with their sound bars clear mental visions of specific kinds of characters. The Dickensian treasury clearly demonstrates the value of names in clothing characters with instant personality to further the stories in which they are featured.

The need for Irish nicknames is most obvious to outsiders who stumble on Gaelic names for the first time. They are most formidable in their original Irish spelling.

A student of Irish nomenclature, Ida Brehan, writes in her book, *Pocket Guide to Irish Family Names (Appletree Press, 1985)* that with the passage of time "nicknames became respectable."

The most common surname in Ireland, Murphy, identifies one in every 75 Irish families. Other common Irish surnames are: Kelly, O'Brien, Sullivan, O'Connor, O'Neill, Byrnes, Reilly, Doyle, Kennedy, Fitzgerald and Walsh. It's an innocent-looking list until you see the original Gaelic spelling. You then begin to appreciate the plight of American customs officials who had to spell out the names of illiterate Irish immigrants on a phonetic basis.

Even the Anglo-Norman invaders fell back in dismay when they were confronted with Irish names. The familiar name of Driscoll, for example, stems out of the Gaelic O'hEidersceoil. Translators first came up with the English version, O'Drisceoil, then O'Driscoll, and finally Driscoll. Many conversions to English were entirely dissimilar. Some samples would include O'Sealbhaigh (Shelly); O Ceileachair (Kelleher), and O Breachain (Grimes).

Modern generations who coin nicknames for their acquaintances are not exactly blazing a new trail. Donough McNamara the Red, an old-time Irish writer, was well-known for the nicknames he fastened on people, as Max Caulfield noted in his book, *The Irish Mystique (Prentice-Hall, 1973)*.

McNamara once listed the teachers of his district as: "Christopher Mac Heavy Bottom; Coxcomb O'Boland; Dirty, Puffy John O'Mulrooney; Giddyhead O'Hackett; Tatter O'Flanagan; Giggler O'Mulcahy, and Blear-eyed O'Cullenan."

In the analysis of any name exists a certain element of mystery, a hint of history that goes deeply into a person's background. The assembled letters of a name may represent simple arrows pointing to all kinds of interesting information about the person.

The names of the Irish offer unusually rich specimens for examination and analysis on all sides, in all climes, because the Irish have spread their surnames and nicknames into virtually every part of the globe, thanks to one painful exodus after another from their small home island. It isn't surprising, for example, that the national hero of Chile is one Bernardo O'Higgins, or that there was a great Spanish general in the 19th century named Leopoldo O'Donnell, or that Cornelius O'Rourke, who settled in Russia, was the father of General Count Joseph Kornilievitch O'Rourke, one of the Russian generals who defeated Napoleon, or that a Uruguayan ambassador to the United States in the past was Eduardo Macgillycuddy himself.

The wild geese who flew from Ireland's shores to escape tyranny and poverty accepted refuge wherever they could, but they usually paid back their benefactor nations in the best way they could, sometimes in roles that won them fame and honor, but more often anonymously through basic, backbreaking hard work that built canals, railroads, buildings and highways.

The basic flaw in this scheme of things was that the same Irish names kept cropping up on all sides. Being relatively few in number, their names were called on to do heavy duty. Indeed, there were so many Irish immigrants named Patrick in early America that the nickname "Paddy" became a generic name for all Irish men and boys.

Imbedded in this practice, to be sure, was an unmistakable rudeness and condescension; the dismissal of lowly immigrants with a common nickname suggesting rather broadly that it was hardly worthwhile to acknowledge their individuality. Willard R. Espy, a leading expert on word origins, noted the same cavalier rejection of true identities of many Irish who bore the names of Michael and Margaret, leading to popular identification of the Irish as 'Micks,' and, in the case of Irish women, as 'Maggies.'"

By way of illustration, during the famous murder trial of Lizzie Borden in Fall River, Mass., in 1892, the accused woman, member of an upper-crust family, continually referred to the household maid as Maggie. The Irish-born servant's proper name was Bridget. Such a minor detail commonly was brushed aside by the social superiors of the immigrants, even by those members of the gentry who stood accused of being axe murderers.

In his book, *O Thou Improper, Thou Uncommon Noun* (Clarkson N. Potter, Publisher, New York) Espy noted other Irish names that were employed in a wider, common generic use. Irish girls, usually serving maids, were downgraded as "biddies," a deprecatory dismissal that started out as the nickname of Bridget. Another example, Mulligan, was an old Irish family name borrowed to describe a meat- and-vegetable stew, also known as Mulligatawny Stew. Murphy was the nickname of the Irish potato, and Seamus (Irish for James) took on new meaning as Shamus, the nickname for a private detective.

The Irish, like other nationalities, have more than a little pride in their names, regarding them as proud badges rather than mere identification tags. The family tree in Ireland is a living organism that is carefully nurtured and kept ever green. The roll call of family names is one that erases time and distance, being a mixture of pride and sentimentality, and even humor, as Journalist Bob Considine discovered in a trip to the land of his forebears in the wartime year of 1943.

In his book, *It's the Irish (Doubleday & Co., N.Y., 1961),* the writer told of his homecoming experience in the company of William Randolph Hearst, jr. The two of them had flown in a Sunderland flying boat from London, stopping in Foynes, Ireland, to refuel on their way to New York.

"The passengers on the plane queued up and inched slowly past the desk of an old gentleman . . . who scrutinized each passport and, upon due deliberation, stamped the edge of a page," wrote Considine. "I was last in line. The old man's impersonal air changed when he read my name. He looked up at me, measuring me in a kindly way, and said one of the dearest things I've ever heard.

"'I was in jail with many a Considine,' he said.

"Several passengers within earshot burst into laughter and the raucous noises they made offended the old man. He silenced them with a glare.

"'It was an honor to be in jail during the T(h)rouble,' he said with great dignity.

"And, of course, he was right. Not to have a jail record was for a long time a handicap for any true Irishman for it implied indifference to a great and glorious crusade for freedom, or, worse, submission to powerful pressures working against that ambition . . . "

Later (wrote Considine) the old man "took me out of the stuffy terminal and pointed across the misty wastes. 'Ennis, in (County) Clare, is over that way,' he said, pointing. 'Your people came from there. Some of them are still in the trees!'"

As that incident illustrated, names have the power to trigger recollections and release the powerful emotions that are encapsulated in our memories. They can bring strangers together or set them apart. They can open doors or cause them to be slammed shut. Some names even have unique powers in themselves, as many contenders for political office have discovered through the years.

All immigrant groups found, upon their arrival in the United States, that the upward social climb in this new land was made easier through the vehicle of politics. Public office in a democracy was within relatively easy reach with ethnic support. People of like nationality boosted each other at the polls, and that was especially true in the case of the Irish in the early years. Politics was a field in which the Gaelic gift of gab and the outgoing nature of the race served the candidates well. Little wonder that to this day election ballots are thick with the names of innumerable Sweeneys, Corrigans, Gallaghers and Kilbanes. That political corridor leading to power also is crowded with other ethnic regulars like Celebreeze, Calabrese, Kovacic, Kovach, Kovachy, Brown and more Browns, Day and more Days. The name game has attracted many players and more than one nationality has found favor with American voters.

*   *   *

Cleveland, Ohio, is as good a place as any to pause in quiet contemplation of the steadily evolving name process, for here it still boils and bubbles away like a misplaced Hawaiian volcano, outwardly dormant at times, but always active under the surface. Newly-coined nicknames, the basic ingredient in the formation of identities, still are being tossed to the surface by people who are not even aware that they are being original and creative.

As a matter of fact, the Irish have coined a nickname for Cleveland itself, it being a city that stands in the forefront of their awareness for very good reasons.

A very high percentage of the many people of Irish descent who live in Cleveland look to County Mayo and, more specifically, its Achill Island, as the place that their ancestors called home.

Kenneth McNally, author of *Achill (David & Charles, Newton Abbot, 1973)* took note of the considerable emigration of so many of the island's people to the Ohio metropolis in his book when he wrote:

"During the famines of last century many emigrants from 'the next parish to America', looking westwards to new worlds across the Atlantic, established little colonies far from their island. Cleveland, Ohio, for example is still nostalgically known as 'Little Achill' among exiles and their families back home."

Cleveland's own name is traceable to an area in the northeastern part of England, once a part of East Yorkshire, renamed Cleveland County in recent years. The principal physical feature of the county is a range of old mountains worn down to the nub by time and the elements and known as the Cleveland Hills. They preside over a countryside marked by clefts, cleaves, or cleves, whose people quite naturally came to be known as clefflanders, or clevelanders. It became the surname of many families, including the ancestors of Moses Cleaveland. When Moses Cleaveland founded a settlement in Connecticut's Western Reserve, he tacked the old nickname on to the site.

The city's reputation for nicknames, novel and numerous, has spread abroad. Name fanciers from distant parts of the world have made pilgrimages to Cleveland over the years in search of fresh nomenclatural (a novel word in itself) sensations, and few of those students were disappointed in their scholarly quest. Cleveland was their Mecca (not to be confused with Medina, a few miles to the south.)

Sad to report, though, there has been a distinct decline in nickname production in Cleveland in recent decades. Indeed, nicknames are on the wane to such an alarming extent that they soon may be classified on the endangered list. The signs are not to be ignored. Not only are thousands of splendid nicknames from the past slipping out of mind as their owners take their final leave, the replacement ratio is below the minimum level needed.

Do-gooders among us who gravely fear the extinction of certain species of hummingbirds and bullfrogs would do well also to rally support for the faltering, limping band of nickname preservationists whose mission is not going well at all, at all.

The way it used to be, any social introduction in Cleveland, especially on the West Side, was a moment of great expectations; one that held the promise of entertainment as well as the enlargement of one's social circle. That hope was realized when you were asked to shake hands with the likes of Bird Legs Boswell, Coal Oil Masterson, or Angel Chambers; but if the introductee didn't have a nickname, it was a definite letdown of a meeting.

"Hello," you said to yourself, "So this is Mike Murphy, is it? And is that all there is to the man? He must be a dull one to have come this far without a nickname."

That seldom happened in the old days. Now it is becoming commonplace as gentrification pursues its damaging course ahead.

Nevertheless, the cognominal heritage is still so highly regarded in many families that nicknames continue to be renewed and perpetuated through descending generations in the same way that nobility passes along its titles in the family line.

Take the way that angels became part of the Chambers family.

When I was a boy growing up on the near West Side, Angel Chambers was a community celebrity. In my childish innocence, I didn't know if he was a politician like Holy Water Mike Gallagher, or a banker like the Feighans but it didn't matter. The appearance of his name on the shirts of the sandlot baseball players at Edgewater Park was proof enough of his importance. The additonal fact that he was an angel certainly didn't hurt his public image.

The original Angel Chambers (it seems) was a boy from Mayo whose true name was Patrick Chambers. One day in childish abandon he skipped school and was wandering in his liberated innocence through a meadow when he was spotted by the headmaster of the school, who was said to have exclaimed (if we are to believe it): "There goes the little angel now!"

Little Paddy Chambers from that day on was known to one and all as Angel. No other name would have done as well. The name hung on even when he grew up and moved to America, to Cleveland, Ohio, in fact.

The important thing to know, as interesting as that background may be, is that when Angel Chambers got married, there were eleven children in his family, six boys and five girls, and every of them, whatever their Christian names, responded to the name of Angel. There was no favoritism in that family.

"We were all angels," agreed Celine Chambers Clark, one of them herself and the wife of none other than Jellybeans Clark.

The history of that family tells a lot about the life of Irish immigrants and their children on the West Side "back in the old days" that really are not that old at all. Their experience was typical. Three of the Chambers boys, John, Patrick and George, took up adult life as tugmen. It was a natural way to go. The tug fleet in Cleveland was manned almost entirely by men from the parishes of St. Malachi's and St. Patrick's.

John (Angel) Chambers, oldest of the three brothers, became president of the tugmen's union. A sports enthusiast, he sponsored amateur baseball and football teams whose Angel Chambers jersies made the West Side that much more interesting and brought him a certain fame in sports circles. But the Chambers family knew tragedy as well as fame. George (Angel) Chambers died when his tug, The Admiral, sank in December, 1942, while towing a barge on a storm-tossed lake.

Another example of a nickname being passed along from one generation to the next is to be found in the Gaul family, established on the West Side at the turn of the century by William Gaul, who, starting with a horse and wagon, built a prosperous hauling business. His son, Francis, was nicknamed "Speed" Gaul when he starred on the football teams of St. Ignatius High School and John Carroll University. The same nickname later was applied to two of Gaul's nephews, Francis and Joseph Gaul; Francis when he played football for Notre Dame, and Joseph when he fought in the Golden Gloves.

The younger Frank Gaul became better known as a politician, serving some 18 years as Cuyahoga County treasurer. His brother Joseph also took the political route, becoming mayor of the suburb of Fairview Park for four terms.

In all fairness, families like the Chambers and the Gauls ought to use Roman numerals after their nicknames in the manner of kings and the popes to keep straight their lineage. There's something quite inspiring in the the very thought of a Speed Gaul III or an Angel Chambers IV.

Most of the old families actually shunned repetition when it came to nicknames. Variety was the order of the day as the pet identifications welled out of the humor that forever bubbled on the neighborhood stove, and even within the family itself. The result naturally was the inside joke, not to be taken literally. Only people who knew the West Side family of Stantons, for example, would appreciate the fact that some nicknames are not all that they seem to be. James "Lazy" Stanton, for example, was the most industrious of men, while his cousin, Patrick "Noisy" Stanton, was a quiet, soft-spoken man.

Because so many nicknames have exactly the opposite meaning, there could be much misunderstanding about them as time goes on, eroding the facts. They would stand as a challenge to social cryptographers who try to unlock the mysteries of the Cleveland scene emerging from the dusty past. The plight of those analysts could be hopeless without a Rosetta Stone to make possible a breakthrough.

It's all very well to be expert at digging up the past, but imagine the confusion of the future scholars when suddenly confronted with a reference in an ancient text to, say, Holy Water Mike? Or Plain Pudd'n Maher? Or Emergency Kelly?

It's unlikely that there would be anybody around to tell the poor, frustrated scholar the facts of West Side life and the stories about the many Gaels there whose names made life more interesting.

*   *   *

The preservation of the historical lore and legend so deeply rooted in nicknames is owed to certain level-headed bystanders who years ago banded together in a common determination to save those nicknames for future generations to admire. They did this not only for their own amusement and sense of historical values, but also to protect the nicknames from the social snobs and the shallow academicians who would dismiss such sobriquets as the foolish word play of the peasantry.

Among those to whom we stand indebted in this cause are some serious-minded collectors, some casual ones with a refined sense of humor, a large number of crusaders against pomposity, and other civic-minded volunteers who many years ago came together in loose confederation, half jokingly, under the ponderous name: The Society to Preserve Irish Nicknames. It is entirely fitting in this age of acronyms that the organization should be familiarly known as SPIN.

Leading members of SPIN to whom we are indebted would include Patrick E. O'Donnell, Manus McCaffery, Francis J. McDonald, Francis J. Talty, William Engel, John Mannix, John J. Donnelly, Thomas L. Sullivan, William Spellacy, Edward Gallagher, Frank J. (Punk) Merrick, Hugh A. Corrigan, Dennis J. McGuire, John P. Butler, John T. Patton, James Patton, Dennis Butler, William (Bill) Roberts, James V. Stanton, Thomas F. Stanton, Don Kelly, James (Jellybeans) Clark, Margaret McCaffery, Patrick Conway, Daniel Conway, Tom Kelly, Thomas Gallagher, Joseph O'Connor, Raymond (Rip) Reilly, Francis Stanton, Marilyn Trepanier, Neil McReynolds, and James Coleman McCoy.

Each of these persons, and others not known, contributed to this rare collection in one way or another. It may be the most complete collection of its kind in Cleveland or any other American city in which Irish colonists gave way to their nicknaming tendencies. Even so, there is the brooding fear, if not the certain knowledge, that some nicknames have been missed, overlooked or forgotten, and that the list includes duplications, misspellings, and other mistakes of omission and commission. 'Twas ever thus.

*   *   *

The central point behind all this profundity is that nicknames should not be judged simply as empty sobriquets, meaningless attempts at humor, or idle japery, even when they are most amusing. Serious students of the subject will find that nicknames sometimes are vessels that carry a full measure of history and tradition, and that even nicknames lacking such content may be justified simply by their power to entertain. That alone, in a frosty-faced world, should make them worth remembering and saving.

An important fact to keep in mind in any review of these names is that each represents a real person, not a fictitious character. Many of the persons listed may be long dead, but their names live on. Dead or alive, as the case may be, they continue to project their personalities through their nicknames, which have the power, collectively, to evoke appreciative smiles from those of us who never knew them but wish that we had.

It's not a minute too soon for the world to join in a toast to this honor roll of old friends and say to them: "Thanks. Without you, there would be less mirth on this old earth."

Mr. Secretary, let the roll call begin.

Getting a Nickname the Hard Way

Walsh was a construction worker who one day fell 30 feet to the ground from the girder of a new building. He didn't bounce, exactly, but he did rise to his feet, shaking his head and brushing himself off, almost immediately. His fellow-workers who had rushed to his side were both relieved and astonished by this demonstration that all of Walsh's vital signs were operating, but they insisted, over his protests, that he lie down and wait to be taken to the nearest hospital.

The injured man scoffed at the advice and refused to allow anybody to call an ambulance or accompany him to the hospital. That was sissy stuff, not for Walsh. Furthermore, there were no emergency ambulances in those days, only police paddy wagons, and he made it clear that a ride in one of those would be an indignity. The wagon was for drunks and criminals. He would take a taxi to the hospital.

"I can take care of myself," he declared. "Call me a cab."

On the way to St. John's Hospital, he ordered the cab driver to stop in front of a saloon and wait for him. With that, he limped into the bar and gulped down a double-header so fast even the bartender's eyes grew moist.

Apparently re-energized by this liquid first-aid, Walsh returned to the cab and resumed his trip to the hospital, where he was immediately bedded for treatment of bruises, lacerations, and all-around fall-itis.

From that day on, Walsh was known to one and all simply as Hardman.

The Waiting Game

There is a collegiality among Irish undertakers that will not be denied. They take life, as well as death, in easy stride.

One day Undertaker Mike Gallagher, a versatile man, was up on the roof of his house, hammering down a few wayward shingles, when he spotted on the street below one of his professional competitors, Dan Berry, sitting at the wheel of his hearse.

"What are you doing down there, Dan?" shouted Gallagher.

"Nothing," answered Berry. "Nothing at all. Just waiting!"

On The Dilemma of a Horn

Hunky Mike Horn, a locomotive engineer by trade, was an Irishman with a talent for foreign accents which were related to no single language anywhere, but which somehow had an authentic ring to them. Out of this grew his nickname. His linguistic talent was one that stood him well in his favorite pastime, that of a professional ribber. In that role, he shattered the composure and patience of thousands of gullible victims.

Mike drove countless victims out their minds at cocktail parties, political rallies, neighborhood bars, and other social settings when he would assume the identity of a foreign-born drunk with a serious leaning toward Communism, an intense dislike of capitalistic bosses, and grave doubts about America—the kind of person, in short, to set any patriot's teeth on edge.

Horn was a master of timing, a vital asset in the life of any professional ribber. Just as his enraged victims began to grope for a weapon to use against him after a long soliloquy on the deficiencies of life in the United States, Horn suddenly would lose his accent and assume a sudden, clear-eyed sobriety that completely threw his listeners off guard. It was a Dr. Jekyll-and-Mr. Hyde performance that was not without its dangers because it often left its victims feeling foolish and, sometimes, still furious.

"The important thing is to stand with your back to the wall," said Horn, advising future ribbers. "You live longer that way."

Holy Water Mike

Among the most popular nicknames in the West Side treasury is that of Holy Water Mike. Its recall stirs enough curiosity to warrant further recollection of the man who, more formally, was Michael Gallagher, a Detroit Avenue undertaker.

Gallagher, whose mortuary was in the vicinity of W. 45th Street on Detroit Avenue, did a brisk business over the years burying any number of West Side Irish, who, in death, as in life, demonstrated a fine sense of Gaelic loyalty in demanding to be interred by One of Their Own. Their patronage was shared through the years by the undertaking establishments of Gallagher, Corrigan, McGorray, Berry, Reidy, Butler, Kilbane, Malloy, and Chambers.

Most of the customers, it goes without saying, would rather die than be buried by a strange undertaker.

Mike Gallagher was prominent early on in this trying field; one in which a mortician has to cope with survivors who usually demand that their departed loved ones look better in death than they ever did in life. What really set Gallagher aside, though, was his graveside technique. It was here that he made a big splash by giving customers a grand finale for their money.

To give the man credit, Mike Gallagher had great forbearance, a most desirable quality in an undertaker. He never allowed himself to be openly unnerved by the keening of the female mourners and the eerie "Irish Cry" that so often arose during the burial ceremony, even though such chilling outbursts normally would be enough to make even the most hardened mortician reach for the smelling salts. But Gallagher, wise in the old ways of the Irish, simply would bow his head and stoically stand his ground, letting the mourners wear themselves out. Not until the clergyman had intoned the final blessing and the crowd was giving the casket one last somber look before its earthward descent would Gallagher step forward and make his big play of the day. In the swiftest of moves that even old-time western gunslingers would have envied, Mike would remove from his inside breast pocket a flask filled with holy water.

Mourners who were veterans of past Gallagher cemetery ceremonies immediately would poise themselves for flight through the tombstones. Those without raincoats raised their bumbershoots high. Then, as the undertaker began to unscrew the cap of the flask, the unprepared looked about for cover. They knew that within seconds he would begin to throw holy water on everything and everybody within splashing range.

Old-time mourners, never the ones to deny a man the credit he deserved, always acknowledged that Mike Gallagher had one of the best throwing arms in the burying business. When he got through pitching, no matter who was being buried, there wouldn't be a dry eye in the crowd, or, for that matter, a dry anything. The holy water did not descend on the people assembled at graveside like the heavenly rain of the soft springtime; it was more like the driven torrent of a hurricane, or the air-borne spume of tropical waves carried on the high winds of a gale.

It was said that after a Gallagher-conducted funeral, the flora, the trees and the bushes of the cemetery immediately took on new life and the grass grew greener than it ever had before. Keep in mind, now, that the water Mike cast about was holy.

Gallagher, by the way, played a dual role in the Ohio City scheme of things. He also was a politician, and in this role represented his ward for many years in Cleveland City council. He won the seat handily, as a rule, and nobody ever accused him of resorting to the dastardly practice of stuffing the ballot box with the names of residents of the cemeteries, although no candidate was better entitled to such support. Political experts will tell you that there isn't too much distance between a mortician and a winning candidate for office. Each usually knows where the bodies are buried.

In one of his re-election campaign speeches, Gallagher promised his constitutents that he would have the city build a public bath house in Fairview Park, on the site of the old Kentucky reservoir between W. 32d Street and W. 38th Street.

Among those in the audience when that promise was made was a thoughtful citizen named Rock Burke, a bridge-tender by occupation, and he was moved to make a point.

"Is it a bath house you'll be building now?" cried out Burke. "Then you'd better have the city build a soap factory alongside it. The voters in this ward need all the lather they can get when they take a bath and your soft soap won't be enough!"

The Day the Cookie Crumbled

Riding a large passenger air liner is never a dull experience, except perhaps among regular business travelers who have lost their sense of awe at being among the clouds above, but there was this Irish priest who always experienced a sense of heightened excitement when he went aloft. Perhaps it was because a flight made him feel closer to God.

There was this day, anyway, when he was waiting to board an airliner to Cleveland at Logan International Airport in Boston, on his way home from a visit to his native County Mayo in Ireland. It had been a happy reunion with some of his relatives and he was still feeling the glow of the visit as he walked through the airport on the way to the gate where he was to board the plane to Cleveland.

He had not been given much time between the arrival of his 747 from Ireland and the time of takeoff for Cleveland; not enough time to buy lunch, certainly, and, being hungry, he was attracted to an airport stand where home-baked chocolate cookies were being sold. It was just what he needed to subdue his appetite until his arrival at the parish house back home, and he bought a dozen cookies.

Better still, the girl behind the counter counted out 13 cookies as she dropped them into a paper bag.

"We give a baker's dozen to our customers," she explained with a smile that made him feel even better about his purchase.

Once aboard the plane, he was directed to the section with three seats across and given the seat closest to the window. The seat in the center was empty. The seat on the aisle was occupied, presently, by a middle-aged, matronly woman. Accompanying her were her three children, who were seated together in the row directly behind her.

The priest was sentimental about children, as most Irish are, but he felt a sense of inner relief over the placement of the woman's offspring to the rear. He was tired from the long ocean flight. Yes, and hungry; in no mood to listen to childish prattle. A little quiet reading time was all he wanted.

He and the mother of the kiddies exchanged polite greetings and then he settled back to read a Boston newspaper as he munched on the first cookie from the bag on the seat between him and the woman. It tasted just as he hoped it would, chewy and chocolatey, and he drew another cookie out of the bag.

To his surprise, and a small stirring of resentment, the woman also reached into the bag and took a cookie. But he didn't say anything. He was not a selfish man and he refused to protest when the same thing happened a few minutes later. He took a cookie and so did she. He still held his silence.

Still and all, it was annoying. Even a man of the cloth is beset by a certain human selfishness, and he found himself fighting down a rising anger which he managed to suppress successfully.

"After all," he told himself, "what's a few cookies?"

But the test continued. When he took his next cookie, the woman continued her plundering. This time, to his disbelief, she took four cookies, kept one and distributed the others to the three children seated behind her.

"What a bold woman she is," thought the priest to himself. "And I'll bet her children are scattering the crumbs all over the seats and the carpeting. No wonder the airlines are having such a difficult time in this day and age. They don't have enough trouble staying in the air, now they've got careless cookie eaters to cope with. And their mother just sits there, cool as a cucumber!"

Realizing now that he was in a competition, he reached for another cookie and it was the same scene all over again. The bold woman again took a handful of cookies; four in all. One for herself and three for the kiddies. His ire had risen to its high point at this critical juncture. There was only one cookie left in the bag.

"I'll be damned if she's going to get my last cookie," said the priest to himself, and he reached for the bag. As he did so, the woman also reached, and her hand went into the bag first. She withdrew the cookie, looked right into the eyes of the priest, wouldn't you know, just as bold as you please, and broke the cookie in two. She gave him one half of his last cookie, bit into her own half, and bent her attention back to the magazine she was reading.

She was so cool and casual about this final division of the goodies that the priest, for some reason, felt as he had been dismissed, as if he no longer had anything to offer.

"It isn't as if I haven't been generous about this whole thing," he told himself. "After all, I only got to eat a few cookies out of the baker's dozen, and she didn't even bother to ask my permission or to say thanks for dipping into my bag. You do meet some strange people when you travel, but I'm glad I held my tongue. There could be a future homily in this."

With that comforting thought, he turned back to his newspaper until the plane landed in Cleveland. When the woman gathered her three children in the aisle and prepared to leave, she looked his way and their eyes met. She nodded her head politely and he nodded back. There was no sense in holding a grudge. Perhaps the poor woman simply didn't know better. The kindly thought made him feel better.

When he arrived at the parish house, the first thing he did was to unpack his briefcase before opening his large traveling bag, and there, in the briefcase, was his bag of chocolate cookies. A baker's dozen of them, no less.

"Damn!" sighed the priest.

He suddenly realized that his bag of cookies had made him swear twice in the same day. Some days are like that.

The Day Steve Brodie Became the Fall Guy

One of America's most famous persons in 1886 was a daring young man named Steve Brodie, a New York newsboy, about whom it was said, "he wanted nothing more in this world than to make front-page headlines in the papers he sold."

The unique, but newsworthy way, in which he realized this ambition and achieved national renown was by jumping from the newly-built Brooklyn Bridge, a high-suspension span that was rightly regarded as one of the world's wonders.

Brodie made the leap from the great bridge 130 feet above the East River on July 23, 1886, and not only lived to tell the tale, he instantly became a national hero. The feat was so highly regarded that his name became part of the language as a synonym for a dangerous jump. To take a "Brodie" was to make an impressive leap off a high place.

Americans, it seems, long have had a weakness for people who are willing to walk on high tight wires or jump off cliffs, bridges, high buildings, waterfalls, or anything else high enough to constitute a risk to life and limb. One of the folk heroes of the early 19th century in upstate New York, for example, was a man named Sam Patch, whose extraordinary careers consisted simply of one jump after another, all to public acclaim.

Sam's outstanding record as a jumper, unfortunately, was marred one winter's day in 1829 when he jumped nicely off the Genessee Falls in Rochester, N. Y., but failed to bob to the surface as expected despite the loud applause. He eventually turned up the following spring as he floated downstream encased in a cake of ice!

The adventurous newsboy, Brodie, made many personal appearances around the country after his leap from the Brooklyn Bridge established him as a celebrity. One of the cities on the tour was Cleveland. Promoters in this city however wanted more than a pirouette and a bow on a theatrical stage from the famous man. They convinced him that the most appropriate way to impress Clevelanders would be with a dive into the Cuyahoga River from the upper deck of the old Superior Viaduct.

Brodie's agreement to this plan showed either the courageous devil-may-care nature of the man or his total ignorance of the condition of the local river. While the viaduct wasn't nearly as high as the Brooklyn Bridge, the Cuyahoga, even in that distant day, was anything but a pellucid waterway. Poets and swimmers alike wisely shunned it, for good reason. The Cuyahoga River then not only was flammable, it was downright explosive, thanks to the use of the river as a dumping ground for one of the waste products of the many refineries that lined its banks. It was a volatile product called gasoline for which no practical use yet had been found.

Any sensible jumper who wanted to make a splash in society would have looked elsewhere. A leap into a vat of boiling wax probably would have been safer. But Brodie agreed to jump from the viaduct.

Entertainment, remember, was hard to come by in 1886 and Cleveland was abuzz with anticipation over the forthcoming event. On the day of the great leap thousands of spectators lined the river banks and milled around the delegation of high-ranking civic leaders who had gathered in the middle of the viaduct for the pre-jump ceremony. Streetcards which normally passed over the bridge every few minutes were held back for the great occasion, while in the river below a large number of small boats clustered as close to the jump zone as they could maneuver. A few boats were rescue craft, in case the jumper had trouble, but most of them simply carried sightseers who wanted a seat up front.

Brodie's appearance on the viaduct evoked a loud round of applause. The daredevil was dressed for the occasion. While bridge-jumping was only on the un-classified fringe of show business, it was undeniably a form of entertainment and a star jumper had to look like something more impressive than the neighborhood banker or the corner grocer. Brodie's costume was so flamboyant as to be entirely appropriate to the heroic occasion. It was a skintight uniform that needed only a large "S" on the chest to be an advance showing of Superman, a Clevelander yet to be invented by a couple of Glenville High School kids named Siegel and Schuster.

A roll of the drums would have been most appropriate when Brodie stepped forward into the full view of the onlookers. When they cheered, he thoughtfully waved an acknowledgment and then nodded his readiness to one of the civic dignitaries wearing a shiny top hat as he advanced to the railing, 68 feet above the Cuyahoga. The crowd held it breath and there was a sudden silence.

It was precisely at that dramatic moment that a small, redheaded boy, no more than 12 years of age, burst out of the crowd of spectators on the viaduct and ran toward the railing a few feet from where Brodie was poised. Before anyone could restrain him, the kid vaulted over the railing and flew out into space.

There were shrieks and cries of alarm from the people on the bridge, but there was no reason for them to fear for the boy's life. This kind of derring-do apparently was old stuff to the kids who lived in the Irish Angle on the western hillside. He descended to the river below in as graceful a swan dive as even the most critical swan-fancier could ask. There was hardly a splash as he spliced the water's surface below, and his shock of red hair was submerged only a matter of seconds before it reappeared. He shook the water from his head like a spaniel coming in from the rain and swam to shore with easy strokes before he scurried off into the hillside of tumbledown shacks that lined the Cuyahoga.

High above, spectators and officials milled about on the deck of the viaduct in a state of total shock over the development. Prepared speeches were hurriedly pocketed and hundreds of extravagant adjectives that had been mobilized for active duty in praise of the expected leap by the hero of the Brooklyn Bridge were returned to inactive status.

Not the least among those who had been surprised by the unscheduled diving display by the unknown kid was Steve Brodie himself. The daredevil performance he was to have provided his admirers obviously had been damaged beyond repair. When a star has been upstaged by a small boy there can be no effective redress. He left the scene in defeat, his cloak wrapped around his heroic frame, and wagging his head in disbelief.

If the program had gone off as scheduled, the Clevelanders on hand would have enjoyed it, without question. But what they had seen mixed humor in with heroism and made it a day even more memorable than expected, especially among the West Side Irish.

Brodie was an Irishman also, true enough, and his Cleveland admirers were proud of his past feats of courage and foolishness, as the case might be, but in this instance one of their very own, a little boy, at that, had stolen the show and given them all something to laugh about in the long nights ahead.

When Bullets Lost the War

Bullets Fox is remembered by friends and admirers as the only man who ever had the nerve or the knowledge to handicap World War II.

He made Germany a 3-point favorite to win the war. Germany lost and so did Bullets, but he insisted later that it was a good gamble.

His Whispers Caught Their Ears

Whispering John Duffy, a familiar figure in City Hall and other public buildings, always carried a cardboard box filled with shirts, socks, and other essential dry goods which he peddled to his select clientele along the way. It's possible he was able to eke out a living through such random salesmanship, but those who knew Duffy well were inclined to believe that the sales effort was no more than a sideline.

Duffy's real love centered on the ponies and the racetrack. Any ponies. Any racetrack. But when he talked about horse racing, his voice, so strident in making a sales pitch, had a way of dropping down to a level that was almost reverential. His listeners had to lean forward and cup their ears to catch what his soft voice was saying. It usually had something to do with the next day's races at Thistledown. Duffy believed wholeheartedly in Theodore Roosevelt's advice to talk softly when you carry a big message.

James E. Doyle, the popular sports columnist of The Plain Dealer, once identified Duffy as "The Dean of Turf Consultants for the West Side," no small distinction.

He was rightly named, Whispering John Duffy was. He proved that a soft voice not only turneth away wrath, it gaineth attention.

Irish Nicknames in Cleveland

A

Fair Weather Adams
Nuisance Adams
Bingy Ahearn
Deafy Allen
Honk Allen
Slick Allen
Buster Andrews
Noisy Andrews
Pans Andrews
Windy Andrews
Stubby Angel
Apples Arthur
Knuckles Arthur
Swibbles Arthur
Jap Austin

B

Shivers and Shakes
  Baker
Bugs Bannon
Bung Bardelheim
Beans Barnes
Bunny Barnes
Fingers Barnes
Midge Barnes
Roach Barnes
Shaker Barnes
Snares Barrett
Tailor Barrett
Bugs Beebe
Oddy Bell
Bugs Belmer
Rinky Bergel
Chick Bergen
Ham Nose Berry
Hoog Berry
Bunion Boland
Fish House Boland
Rube Bond
Fullweight Bonham
Bird Legs Boswell
Side Saddle Bowen
Brainy Bowers
Six-of-a-Kind Boyle
Skunkie Breen
Bottles Brennan
Gauzy Brennan
Red Brennan
Button Briggs
Soldier Brock
Pope Brock

Rocky Burke
Rodney Burke
Scotty Burke
Single-Bed Burke
Turkey Burke
Artillery Burns
Boosey Burns
Button Nose Burns
Cuppy Burns
Dimes Burns
Farmer Burns
Melody Burns
Ichabod Butler
Phantom Butler

C

Moose Broderick
Wigs Broderick
Left-Shoulder-Up
   Buckley
Tit Brogan
Arab Burke
Bulky Burke
Cussie Burke
Darby Burke
Dixie Burke
Dobbins Burke
Flop Burke
Gobble Burke
Gug Burke
Haddock Head Burke
Johnnie Boy Burke
Little Boy Blue Burke
Pat-the-Arab Burke

Doddsy Cahill
Booger Caddick
Midge Cahill
Pork Cahill
Tickle-Toe Cahill
Yank Cahill
Brandy Cain
Buck Cain
Bummer Cain
Dodger Cain
Dorando Cain
Greeny Cain
Idle Cain
Newspaper Joe Cain
Sugar Cain
Trumpet Cain
Whiskers Cain

Doe Cain
Soldier Caine
Puffy Caldwell
Bash Callahan
Brute Callahan
Peggy Callahan
Pope Callahan
Puddy Callahan
Yaw-Yaw Calvey
Guvna Calvin
Jackie Campbell
Big Maude Campbell
Painsey Campbell
Sharkey Campbell
Sweet Lips Campbell
Timber Leg Campbell
Uncle Owen Campbell
Volunteer Campbell
Gigi Carey
Mother Carey
Packy Carey
Sergeant Cargill
Jumbo Carlin
Cowboy Carlin
Monk Carlin
Noisy Carlin
Slixty Slix Carlin
Lum Carlin
Butch Carney
Maximum John
   Carney
Winky Carpenter
Greeney Carr
Nig Carr

Whiskers Carr
Backyard Casey
Oyster Eye Casper
Fats Cavanaugh
Leather Cavanaugh
Nuts Cavney
Angel Chambers
Billy Whiskers
   Chambers
Brickyard Chambers
Broad Belt Chambers
Ghost Chambers
Heinie Chambers
Ice Cream Chambers
Lambie Chambers
Lay Down Chambers
Packie Chambers
Plank Chambers
Scatter Brains
   Chambers
Shorty Chambers
Sitdown Chambers
Skans Chambers
Skins Chambers
Snoot Chambers
Standup Chambers
Stonewall Chambers
Sub Chambers
Sunshine Chambers
Zillie Chambers
Ax Christener
Pug Christener
Banjo Claffey
Batty Clark

Huckleberry Clark
Jellybeans Clark
Oyster Eye Clark
Belfry Cleary
Candy Maker Cleary
Cook Cleary
Dolly Cleary
Dumpy Cleary
Happy Days Cleary
Muscle Cleary
Salamander Cleary
Snitch Cleary
Spike Cleary
Fish Cody
Curls Coleman
Moose Coleman
Bubble Colligan
Cokey Collins
Fatty Collins
Fiddle Back Collins
Mousey Collins
Pale Face Collins
Piggy Collins
Popeye Collins
Slant Eyes Collins
Spinney Collins
Skinny Collins
Skinny Comer
Cutie Connors
Doggy Connors
Moxie Connors
Plump Connors
Touchy Connors
Toots Conroy
Fat Conway

Mocky Conway
Roofer Conway
Rooster Cook
Shirttail Cook
Two Thumbs Cook
Bighead Cooney
Boots Cooney
Piano Legs Cooney
Stirabout Cooney
Tipper Cooney
Tipps Cooney
Tubbs Cooney
White Wings Cooney
Tittie Corkill
Pinky Corlett
Boston Corrigan
Butt Straps Corrigan
Fair Play Corrigan
False Face Corrigan
Fire Eye Corrigan
Fishy Corrigan
Gentleman Jack
    Corrigan
Good Eye Corrigan
Goose Corrigan
Hawker Corrigan
Honey Corrigan
Hugger Corrigan
Husky Corrigan
Initial Corrigan
Mad Dog Corrigan
Mitty Achill corrigan
More Skins Corrigan
Pat-the-Shovel
    Corrigan

Peachy Corrigan
Polish Patty Corrigan
Skeez Corrigan
The Captain Corrigan
The Lieutenant
    Corrigan
Zip Cotter
Boy-Boy Coughlin
Curly Coughlin
Girlie Coughlin
Shadow Coughlin
Toodles Coughlin
Black Martin Coyne
Babe Crane
Taffy Crawford
Double Crawley
Ikey Cronin
Goo-Goo Crowley
Ripper Cullitan
Cooney-Up
    Cunningham
Hoogy Curtain
Retroactive Cusick

D

Blackjack Dare
Fat Jack Dare
Chief Daugherty
Spook Daugherty
Botch Davison
Muzzie DeGrandis
Buttsey Dehaney
Dada Dehaney
Monk Dehaney

Nappy Delmore
Dutch Dempsey
Hombo Dempsey
Divvie DeVaughn
Short Vincent Deveny
Comical Dever
Kugo Dever
Moocher Dever
Mushy Dever
Waltz-Me-Around-
    Again-Willie Dever
Curley Devereaux
Sparky DiBenedetto
Moxie Divis
Spitzy Dolan
Brandy Donahue
Jiggs Donahue
Coosem Donelan
Monk Donelan

Double ("D.D.")
  Donnelly
Molly-the-Doctor
  Donnelly
Butter Doran
14 Doran
Friggy Doran
Six O'Clock Dorsey
B. D. Dowling
Bummer Doyle
Dokes Doyle
Longshoreman Doyle
Red Handle Jack Boyle
Full Eight Duffy
Shovel Duffy
Whispering John Duffy
Bad Eye Dugan
Banana Dugan
Binn Dugan
Bugadee Dugan
Cheesey Dugan
China Dugan
Digger Dugan
Doodles Dugan
Hard Hat Dugan
Jinto Dugan
Oheey Dugan
Red Eye Dugan
Skinny Dugan
Sulky Dugan
Soot Dunn
Strawberry Dunn
Turkey Durkin
Jazz Dwyer

Mushy Dwyer
Shanks Dwyer
Sheenie Dwyer
Skip Dwyer
Balky Dye

E

Babe Early
Tickle Eastwood
Dee Ebenger
Tip Egan
Rotten Gut Eilert
Horseface Ellsworth
Snorts Ellsworth
Dutch Emmons
Brute English
Cloggy English
Mickey English
Pinhead English
Pounder English
Punta English
Seaney English
Skinner English
Tanks English
Dippy Evans
Hobo Evans
Ownie Evans

F

Etcheen Fallon
Pagan Fallon

Coal Oil Farley
Honest John Farley
Finkey Farrow
Fiddle Face Farry
Bootsy Fay
Stinky Fay
Bowery Feeley
Cigars Feeley
Muckel Feeley
Banker Feighan
Mickey Feeney the
    Night Mayor
Custy Fergus
Hopper Fergus
Squarehead Fergus
Pope Fielding
Bliz Finn
Dubb Finn
Peanuts Finnegan
Shirttail Finnerty
Squirrel Finnerty
Fuzzy Finucan
High Pockets
    Fitzgerald
Lighthouse Fitzgibbons
Bidda Flaherty
Honest John Fleming
Big Bill Fletcher
Long Tom Flynn
Porky Flynn
Pueblo Flynn
Si Flynn
Suitcase Sammy Flynn
Tugboat Flynn

Dewey-the-Dancer
    Forrest
Pookie Forrest
Saucer Forrest
Shimsey Forrest
Curbstone Foster
Slugs Foster
Bullets Fox
Dude Frey
Cotton Top Frisch
Bowser Froelich
Buster Froelich

G

Bad Jack Gallagher
Balls Gallagher
Bananas Gallagher
Beer Belly Gallagher
Big Gus Gallaghe
Black Jack Gallagher
Blossom Gallagher
Bobo Gallagher
Boo Gallagher
Butch Gallagher
Corky Gallagher
Dancer Gallagher
Dead Arm Gallagher
Digger Gallagher
Dimie Gallagher
Docko Gallagher
Donuts Gallagher
Double-Breasted
    Gallagher

Drip Gallagher
Ducky Gallagher
Dutch Gallagher
Dyke Gallagher
Farmer Gallagher
Fathead Gallagher
Fudge Gallagher
Geezer Gallagher
Hardback Gallagher
Hay Belly Gallagher
Hazel Gallagher
Holy Water Mike
 Gallagher
Jiggs Gallagher
Kettle Gallagher
Lady Killer Gallagher
Leather Gallagher
Mailer Gallagher

Moneybags Gallagher
Moon Gallagher
Nig Gallagher
Nuts Gallagher
Packy Gallagher
Patcheen Gallagher
Patsy Tank Gallagher
Phwat's-Your-Name
 Gallagher
Pothead Gallagher
Rats Gallagher
Red Jack Gallagher
Salt Box Gallagher
Silk Shirt Gallagher
Slasher Gallagher
Slick Gallagher
Socks Gallagher
Soxie Gallagher
Tallow Gallagher
Tailor Gallagher
Tank Gallagher
Tea Gallagher
Tickets Gallagher
Toots Gallagher
Truthful Gallagher
Wakehouse Charlie
 Gallagher
Whiskers Gallagher
Worms Gallagher
Plumber Gannon
Burkey Garrity
Harp Garrity
Old Man Garrity
Chucker Garvey

Crackers Gaughan
Augie Gaul
Speed Gaul
Booby Gavin
Brick Gavin
Chalk Gavin
Geever Gavin
Patcheen Gavin
Pug Gavin
Chalk Gee
Butch Geiger
Sharp Axe Gerard
Gabby Gerrity
Grit Gerrity
Monk Gerrity
Gib Gibbons
Hoot Gibbons
Jaybird Gibbons
Milo Gibbons
Perk Gibbons
Scotch Gibbons
Booby Giblin
Calico Eye Gilby
Onions Gillespie
Spot Gillespie
Scotty Gilmour
Ballast Ginley
Boob Ginley
Clew Bay Ginley
Dee Ginley
Drum Head Ginley
Duke Ginley
Gedge Ginley
Happy Ginley

Hocker Ginley
Kaiser Ginley
Patney Ginley
Scrapper Ginley
Spas Ginley
Spasm Ginley
Specs Ginley
Two Thumbs Ginley
Wan Ginley
Spook Gleason
Spot Golding
Heinie Goldman
Yocko Goldman
Chief Gordon
Believe-U Gorman
Bow-Wow Gorman
Boxer Gorman
Butts Gorman
Game Gorman
Headlight Gorman
Judge Gorman
Sharkie Gorman
Sheeny Gorman
Tug Gorman
Twitter Gorman
Herkey Grace
Peanuts Grady
Tommy-Tommy Two-
   Tail Grady
Baldy Graham
Long Drawers Graves
Curly Grealis
Itchy Grealis
Boze Green

Blue Belly Yankee
  Gross
Poots Gross
Unk Gundelak
Bunch Gunn

H

Hicky Haak
Skull Haak
Butch Haggerty
Shorty Haggerty
Hockey Haley
Pickle Barrel Haley
Biddy Hall
Bootsy Hall
Hap Halligan
Weak Eyes Hallis
Biddy Halloran
John-the-Bag
  Hamilton
Biddie Hammon
Flat Haney
Paddy-the-Bug Haney
Acey Haney
Bottles Hannon
Mugsie Hannon
Cinder Hansen
Junior Hanton
Deacon Haswell
Skeeter Hatch
Bully Hayes
Stinky Hayes
Deedee Haylor

Mare Hazeltine
Squeaky Hazelton
Yellow Heagle
Hockey Healey
Deacon Hearns
Hopper Hearns
Slugger Hearns
Dudey Heff
Dude Heffron
Knobby Hegan
Bluenose Heller
Gunner Henahan
Sandy Henahan
Spike Hennessey
Dutch Henry
Harky Herald
Humpy Higgins
Lip Higgins
Dutch Hinkle
Squirts Hinkle
Bullets Hoard
Soxsie Hoban
Blinky Hobson
Bunkie Hobson
Bunkie Hogan
Chaw Hogan
Schmosh Hogan
Crackhead Holmes
Head-and-a-Half
  Holmes
Split Lips Holmes
Tug Holmes
Toilet Water Holtzman
Rin-Tin-Tin Hopkins

Up-and-Down Hopkins
Bag-a-Rag Horn
Hunky Mike Horn
Horky Horvath
Red Hoynes
Kicker Hudson
Ape Hughes
Breeze Hurley
Rip Hurley
Satchel Hurley
Thumbs-Up Hurley
Apples Hutchins
Judge Hutchins
Squeak Hutchins

J

Honey Dumper Jacobs
Satchel James
Hap Jenkins
Splunk Jennings
Happy Johnson
Lala Jones
Bailey Joyce
Bat Air Joyce
Bugs Joyce
Caesar Joyce
Donkey Joyce
Flop Joyce
Gin Arm Joyce
Gunner Joyce
Hard-as-Nails Joyce
Jakey Joyce
Jewels Joyce

Jockey Joyce
Jumbo Joyce
Leakey Joyce
Miller Joyce
Pipes Joyce
Poopy Joyce
Red Nose Mike Joyce

K

Bomber Kane
Brandy Kane
Brocky Kane
Bummer Kane
Cohn Kane
Deadwood Kane
Greeny Kane
Idle Kane

Invincible Kane
Soldier Kane
Star Kane
Tired Kane
Whiskers Kane
John-the-Broom Keane
Bird Legs Keating
Fiddler Keating
Homer Keating
Scratch Keaton
Doodles Keegan
Boots Keese
Potato Face Keller
Bad Eye Kelly
Baldo Kelly
Belly Kelly
Belly Laugh Kelly
Bluther Kelly
Buck Kelly
Buckles Kelly
Budka Kelly
Chief Kelly
Dobbins Kelly
Emergency Kelly
Giggle Kelly
Good Eye Kelly
Good Fun Kelly
Honest John Kelly
Midge Kelly
Rockport Kelly
Salt Kelly
Sandwich Kelly
Spider Kelly
Bowser Kennedy
Irish Kennedy

Ding-Dong Kenny
Black Jack Kerrigan
Dash Kerrigan
Fishy Kerrigan
Shin-Legs Kerrigan
Punchy Kessner
Armistice Kilbane
B. S. Kilbane
Baldie Kilbane
Black Bernie Kilbane
Blackie Kilbane
Breezy Kilbane
Broadway Mick
   Kilbane
Bumble Bee Kilbane
Bumpy Kilbane
Butch Kilbane
Chick Kilbane
Fair Play Kilbane
Gallus Kilbane
Gigi Kilbane
Good Lookin' Kilbane
Handsome Kilbane
Husky Kilbane
Ice Wagon Kilbane
Ikey Kilbane
Kibo Kilbane
Killer Kilbane
Killy Kilbane
Lady Kilbane
Lady-Killer Kilbane
Lefty Kilbane
Mihall More Kilbane
Mopey Kilbane
Nig Kilbane

Nit Kilbane
Pickles Kilbane
Popsy Kilbane
Porky Kilbane
Punta Kilbane
Red Bernie Kilbane
Shauneen Kilbane
Snobs Kilbane
Sport Kilbane
Stoney Kilbane
Taffy Pockets Kilbane
Toothpick Kilbane
Upon-My-Word
    Kilbane
Chiney Kilcoyne
Dippy Kilcoyne
Mulraney Kilcoyne
Shawn Kilcoyne
Shoot-th-Hat Kilcoyne
Splring Heel Kinney
Dublin Dan Kirwin
Rock Knoble
Red Kuntz

L

Frenchie Laland
Chunk Lalonde
They-Sent-For-Me
    Larrigan
Yankee Pete Larson
Ambitious Lavelle
Black John Lavelle
Bull-of-the-Woods
    Lavelle

Codger Lavelle
Conger Lavelle
Coxey Lavelle
Duck Lavelle
Freckles Lavelle
Goose Lavelle
Hook Lavelle
Mikey-the-Boat Lavelle
Mock Lavelle
Natural Stiff Lavelle
Pope Lavelle
Red John Lavelle
Rubber Lines Lavelle
Shy Lavelle
Bo Lavine
Bottles Lavine
Butch Lavine
Musty Lawlor
Chit Lee
Cowboy Lee
Dukie Lee
Crab Lennon
Ticklo Leonard
Buddha Lewis
Scrubby Lewis
Toughy Lind
Paddy Livingstone
Cue Ball Lloyd
Dutch Loeb
Cappy Loftus
Horse-and-Buggy
    Loftus
Peejay Logan
Skinner Logan
Bum Lothian

Chisel-Chin Lowry
Cracker Lynch
Egghead Lynch
Fake Lynch
Jughead Lynch
Peggy Lynch
Smich Lynch
Spiney Lynch
Sucky Lynch
Tilda Lynch
Goggles Lyons
Shiney Lyons
Skinny Lyons

M

Speakeasy Mack
Specs Mack
Tony Mack

Biz Mackey
Wacky Mackey
Boss Madden
Gee Madden
Judge Madden
Pants Madden
Peg-Leg Madden
Slim Madden
Champ Madigan
Slip Madigan
Blondie Magnusson
Plain Pudd'n Maher
Wootsie La Maher
Rabbit Mahon
Deadman Mahoney
Push Malady
Boozer Malloy
Ciggy Malloy
Clod Malloy
Crab Malloy
Digger Malloy
Foggy Malloy
Hairpin Malloy
Hard Hat Malloy
Jags Malloy
Mickey-the-Dog
   Malloy
Midge Malloy
No-Show Malloy
Paddy Malloy
Peck Malloy
Primrose Malloy
Pudgy Malloy
Rooster Malloy

Shake-and-Bake
    Malloy
Shep Malloy
Shoulder-the-Wind
    Malloy
Silver Vest Malloy
Hiker Malone
Bizzy Mancuso
I'll-Have-the-Same
    Maney
Beardy Mangan
Comical Mangan
Count Mangan
Dinky Mangan
Greasy Mangan
Heels Mangan
Rabbi Mangan
Scrape-the-Pot
    Mangan
Red Manning
Fat Jack Mare
Rube Marquard
Bar Marsden
Canuck Martlock
Bat Masterson
Blackie Masterson
Blindy Masterson
Bootsie Masterson
Brick Masterson
Brockey Masterson
Bulldog Masterson
Canuck Masterson
Chesty Masterson
Coal Oil Masterson

Connie Masterson
Cousin Frank
    Masterson
Duckie Masterson
Fat Masterson
Flunky Masterson
Ginger Masterson
Honey Masterson
Honorable John
    Masterson
Jap Masterson
Judge Masterson
Knobby Masterson
Beers Masterson
Knob Head Masterson
Lousy Masterson
Paugeen Masterson
Piggy Masterson
Porrick Masterson
Red Maudie Masterson
Rocky Masterson
Schmuck Masterson
Smacker Masterson
Sport Masterson
Sprouts Masterson
Spuds Masterson
Squeaky Masterson
Squint Masterson
Squirt Masterson
Stumps Masterson
Tiger Masterson
Tomasch Masterson
Wackie (The Judge)
    Masterson

Packy Meaney
Punk Merrick
Wee Wee Metzger
Smiler Miles
Bootsy Miller
Monkey Miller
Scrap Iron Miller
Brillo Minillo
Banana Mitchell
Salty Moher
Midgy Moher
Sport Monahan
Stuffy Monroe
Ockey Moody
Boob Moran
Bugs Moran
Cockeye Moran
Crow's Feet Moran
Gamie Moran

Gooney Moran
Goose Moran
Jughead Moran
Lefty Moran
Nid Eye Moran
Blinky Morgan
Spook Morgan
Piggy Morrison
Flukey Morrison
Spuds Morrison
Rollicking Bill Mulcahy
Classy Muldoon
Pick Mulhall
Pickles Mulhall
Pinky Mulhall
Toot Mulhall
Jose Mulhauser
Packy Mullin
Dude Mullins

Now It Can Be Told

When a friend, overcome by nostalgia, asked John McAdams whatever happened to all the Irish who used to live in the Angle, he received a ready reply.

"They all moved to Rocky River and became Republicans," answered McAdams.

Pippy Mullins
Wingy Mullins
Authority Mulran
Brawss Munhall
Apples Muntean
Bee Murphy
Big Tom Murphy
Big Wages Murphy
Clown Murphy
Count-the-Nickels
   Murphy
Cup Cakes Murphy
Devil Murphy
Donkey Pete Murphy
Eastern Murphy
Farts Murphy
Hand Axe Murphy
Iron Horse Murphy
Ky Murphy
Legro Murphy
Little Tom Murphy
Paddle Foot Murphy
Plaster Murphy
Raincoat Murphy
Rough House Murphy
Sanitary Murphy
Single Bed Murphy
Skeets Murphy
Snapper Murphy
Snipe Murphy
Soldier Murphy
Spud Murphy
Starch Murphy

Tombstone Murphy
Turk Murphy
Big Wages Murray
Bluther Murray
Buckets Murray
Bullet Murray
Handle Bar Murray
Mickey-th-Boy Murray
Moocher Murray
Moon Eyes Murray
Mucho Murray
Mugsy Murray
Packy Murray
Roddy Murray
Roughy Murray
Roundhouse Murray
Shanty Murray

Snoot Murray
Squinty Murray
Wise Mike Murray

Mc

Bagears McAdams
Lover McAdams
Boots McAllister
Nuisance McAllister
Sport McAllister
Buffalo McAlpine
Splints McArdle
Let's-You-Give-Me-a-
    Chance McBride
Hard Hat McCaffery
Tricky Mickey
    McCaffery
Babe McCafferty
Breakaway McCafferty
Bunts McCafferty
Big Foot McCafferty
Grasshopper
    McCafferty
Hill Roaming Jake
    McCafferty
Hobble Schwabble
    McCafferty
Jate McCafferty
Jumbo McCafferty
Pork Chops McCafferty
Pot Head McCafferty
Scratch McCafferty
Stubby McCalvey

Bunchy McCann
Dirty Shirt McCann
Fill Up McCann
Goosey McCann
Shirt McCann
Shoo-Fly McCann
Truth McCann
Adjuster McCarthy
Agate Nose McCarthy
Big Words McCarthy
Black Cat McCarthy
Bossy McCarthy
Brick McCarthy
Chick McCarthy
Cow Face McCarthy
Fire Plug McCarthy
Five Yards McCarthy
Gin-for-Mine McCarthy
Gunner McCarthy
Head-and-a-half
    McCarthy
Jiffy McCarthy
Knapsack McCarthy
Lantern Jaw McCarthy
Ockey McCarthy
Pickles McCarthy
Press McCarthy
Pickles McConnell
Polish McConnell
Red McConnell
Codger McCridden
Fox McCrone
Hawker McCrone
Legs McCune

Punk McCrystal
Boggs McDermott
Bot McDermott
Bunter McDermott
Caesar McDermott
Camp McDermott
Dutch McDermott
Giggle McDermott
Jumbo McDermott
Mop McDermott
Big Beers McDonald
Dude McDonald
Maucheen McDonald
Silver Heels McDonald
Spareribs McDonald
Yatsy McDonald
Pickles McDonnell
Polish McDonnell
Red McDonnell
Squint McDonnell
Tankey McDonnell
Fast Horse McFadden
Fats McFadden
Fejo McFadden
Gas Gas McFadden
Goo Goo McFadden
Great Scott McFadden
Lawyer McFadden
Pipes McFadden
Point McFadden
Slats McFadden
Slim McFadden
Blinky McFarland
Red McFaul

Rabbits McGaff
Shoe-Fly McGann
Susie McGeever
Pot Eye McGilly
Bible McGinty
Blackjack McGinty
Block McGinty
Canny McGinty
Duke McGinty
Fur Belly McGinty
Girlie McGinty
Hair McGinty
Max McGinty
Michael-the-Crutch
    McGinty
Mickey McGinty
Mosey McGinty
Moxie McGinty
Ownie Chops McGinty
Ownie Girlie McGinty
Parson McGinty
Patter McGinty
Rabbi McGinty
Rockport McGinty
Sailor McGinty
Sharkie McGinty
Silver Vest McGinty
Smiler McGinty
Spit-on-the-Hands
    McGinty
Stutter McGinty
Sultan McGinty
Swift McGinty
Tadder McGinty

Yoker McGinty
Schwartz McGoey
Chalk Eye McGovern
Ear Rings McGovern
Sphinx McGovern
Guv McGrael
Doll Eyes McGrail
Bugsy McGraw
Ownie-Girlie McGraw
Scratch McGraw
Mugsy McGraw
Fat McGruder
Deacon McGuire
Scotty McGuire
Peanuts McGuire
Moocher McGushin

Donkey McHall
Hurry-Up McInerny
Stuffy McInnis
Moxie McInty
Budge McIntyre
Buggie McIntyre
Bunts McIntyre
Butch McIntyre
Champ McIntyre
Chump McIntyre
Clump McIntyre
Dogs McIntyre
Iggie McIntyre
Lippy McIntyre
Moxie McIntyre
Our Will McIntyre
Red McIntyre

Tady McIntyre
Half-a-Lawyer McKain
Big Words McLaughlin
Bugs McLaughlin
Darby McLaughlin
Facey McLaughlin
Faith-He-Had
    McLaughlin
Foggy McLaughlin
Geekers McLaughlin
Goggle McLaughlin
Kayo McLaughlin
Mockel McLaughlin
Moocher McLaughlin
Mother McLaughlin
Roughie McLaughlin
Rugby McLaughlin

Scotty McLaughlin
Sneakers McLaughlin
Spats McLaughlin
Strawberry
    McLaughlin
Biggie McMahon
Rubbers McMahon
Dogs McManamon
Fiddler McManamon
Tiger McManamon
Tom-the-Dog
    McManamon
Specksie McManamon
Sleepy Hollow
    McNaughton
Brute McNeff
Bugs McNeil
Curley McNeil
Engine McNeeley
Heels McNeeley
Railroad Joe McNeeley
Sandpike McNeeley
Slick McNeeley
Whistler McNeeley
Mickey-the-Buzz
    McNeeley
Boots McNulty
Champ McNulty
Diggie McNulty
Doakes McNulty
Froggy McNulty
Lead McNulty
Rags McNulty

Smoke McNulty
Short Sleeves McNulty
Mother McReady
Connie McReynolds
Chimes McSherry
Chimp McSherry
Deutsch McSweeney
Hunch McSweeney
Tag McTaggart
Chalky McTighe
Schwartzy McTighe
Bull McTigue
Darby McTigue
High Water McTigue
Junk McTigue
Lead McTigue
Prunes McTigue
Sambo McTigue
Schwartz McTigue

N

Gitch Nealing
Hickey Nealon
Brutus Needham
Gara Needham
Redney Needham
Tootler Needham
Tuddy Needham
Scotch Nellie
Limey Newell
Blackfoot Nolan
Empty Head Nolan

Shivers Nolan
Snub Nolan
Spud Nolan
Weasel Nolan
Yockaday Nolan

O

Blue O'Boyle
Butter O'Boyle
Cooper O'Boyle
Hank O'Boyle
Navy O'Boyle
Red O'Boyle
Shanks O'Boyle
Six-of-a-Kind O'Boyle
Whitey O'Boyle
Yelly O'Boyle
Darby O'Brien
Grab-Bag O'Brien
Scabby O'Brien
Tug O'Brien
Connie O'Connell
Amen O'Donnell
Buckskin O'Donnell
Bullet O'Donnell
Burr Head O'Donnell
Butch O'Donnell
Chase O'Donnell
Cinder-Eye O'Donnell
Click O'Donnell
Connie O'Donnell
Double O'Donnell
Goose O'Donnell

Greaser O'Donnell
Ike O'Donnell
Jump O'Donnell
Little O'Donnell
Paldado O'Donnell
Pickles O'Donnell
Red O'Donnell
Sass O'Donnell
Scrap O'Donnell
Screw O'Donnell
Shack O'Donnell
Squint O'Donnell
Yallie O'Donnell
Yatsie O'Donnell
Yawley O'Donnell
Mike-the-Sweep
  O'Hara
Bananas O'Malia
Battling Tom O'Malia
Blubber O'Malia
Bundary O'Malia
Gas House O'Malia
Last Word O'Malia
Nitty Naughty O'Malia
Pudd'n O'Malia
Akka Bakka O'Malley
Auogeen O'Malley
Barstool O'Malley
Big Beers O'Malley
Blubber O'Malley
Brassie O'Malley
Brownie O'Malley
Buddy O'Malley
Conger O'Malley

Crack O'Malley
Crappie O'Malley
Curver O'Malley
Dago O'Malley
Filthy O'Malley
Foam O'Malley
Gas House O'Malley
Green Stamps
    O'Malley
Grimsey O'Malley
Growler O'Malley
Gubbers O'Malley
Hiker O'Malley
Hipsey O'Malley
Hoodak O'Malley
Horse O'Malley
Honest John O'Malley
Jarback O'Malley
John-the-Liar O'Malley
John-the-Undertaker
    O'Malley
Joe Bawn O'Malley
Josie Joe Bawn
    O'Malley
Junior O'Malley
Latch O'Malley
Lawyer O'Malley
Lefty O'Malley
Loophole O'Malley
Loud Laugh O'Malley
Midge O'Malley
Monk O'Malley
Nish O'Malley
Nobby O'Malley

Ouch O'Malley
Patsy Balls O'Malley
Patsy Bolivar O'Malley
Patsy Josie O'Malley
Printer O'Malley
Scotty O'Malley
Shirttail O'Malley
Shonicker O'Malley
Sleepy John O'Malley
Sneaker O'Malley
Socker O'Malley
Sonny O'Malley
Speedy O'Malley
Squint O'Malley
Sties O'Malley
Stinky O'Malley
Track O'Malley
Windy Gap O'Malley

Yance O'Malley
Yukon O'Malley
Broad O'Neill
Bunk O'Neill
Copper O'Neill
Hop O'Neill
Hud O'Neill
Little Liquor O'Neill
Monk O'Neill
Pug O'Neil
Red O'Neil
Step-and-a-Half
   O'Neill
Tip O'Neill
Jilager O'Rourke
Mouse O'Rourke
Alley Owens
Liverlip Owens

P

Shorty Palm
Dode Paskert
Mad Dog Patterson
Slap-the-Goose
   Patterson
Banjo Patterson
Beak Patton
Blinker Patton
Bronco Patton
Bugsy Patton
Doc Patton
Dode Patton
Duck Patton
Filcheen Patton

Fight Gone Patton
Forty Suits Patton
Gussie Patton
Harpo Patton
Hood Up Patton
Hummer Patton
Hump Patton
Johnny Bull Patton
King Patton
Klondike Patton
Mahoxie Patton
Martin-the-Goose
   Patton
Melodian Patton
Midget Patton
Mockey Patton
Mountain Goat Patton
Nanny Goat Patton
Navy Patton
Painter Patton
Patcheen Patton
Peaky Patton
Pest Patton
Poo-Poo Patton
Poschke Patton
Red John Patton
Shawn Rue Patton
Shimmy Patton
Silver Patton
Sitting Bull Patton
Skin-the-Cat Patton
Sliver Patton
Snipes Patton
Soldier Patton
Tit-for-Tat Patton

Tough Patton
Tougher Patton
T'Other Patton
Tumblety Patton
Dee Dee Pischel
Biff Powers

Q

Duty Quinn

R

Pet Rawlings
Pope Leo Ray
They-Give-Me-Too-
    Much Ray
Nobby Reagan
By Gollies Reddy
Coke Reddy
Corn Cob Reddy
Dooley Reddy
Granola Reddy
Lovey Reddy
Moocher Reddy
Nig Reddy
Pinhead Reddy
Mullet Reilly
Rip Reilly
Time Card Reilly
Yance Reilly
Chezzie Reynolds
Iggie Reynolds
Roscoe Reynolds
Sarge Reynolds

Bicycle Riley
Buz Riley
Wee-Wee Riley
Toper Roche
Unk Roche
Little Moe Rooney
Moe Rooney
Chief Ruddy
Lew-the-Fighter Ruddy
Bananas Ryan
Congo Ryan
Gamey Ryan
Giblets Ryan
Mambo Ryan
Parson Ryan
Rammer Ryan
Sassafrass Ryan
Shipyard Ryan
Slippery Ryan
Squirt Ryan
Tish Ryan
Toe Bunker Ryan
Wise Mike Ryan
Zanko Ryan

S

Bart Sadler
Leakers Sallot
Chatterbox Sammon
Donblow Sammon
Jobsy Sammon
Gunkey Sammon
Noggle Sammon
Rackets Sammon

Brandy Sanders
Brick Sanders
Squint Sanders
Pinky Schulte
Long Tom Sexton
Bugs Shannon
Duck-on-the-Rock
   Shannon
Pinch Bar Shannon
Scrib Shannon
Jap Sheardon
Tank Sherman
Swami Sikkil
Bighead Sinclair
Dude Simmons
Nuts Singleton
Peachie Singleton
Snoze Singleton

Splutter Singleton
Spoon Singleton
Sprat Singleton
Big Smith
Bim Smith
Biscuits Smith
Button Mouth Smith
Divil Smith
Porthole Smith
Pug Smith
Red Smith
Schneider Smith
Blimp Snyder
High Collar Snyder
Bump Stafford
Crutch Stafford
Goosey Stafford
Hooks Stafford
Hump Stafford
Kutch Stafford
Stalebread Staley
Axle Stanton
Black Mike Stanton
Buckeye Stanton
Bumpsy Stanton
Bunky Stanton
Chick Stanton
Copperhead Stanton
44 Stanton
88 Stanton
Fleety Stanton
Give Me Stanton
Gunner Stanton
Heel-and-Toe Stanton

Lazy Stanton
Long Martin Stanton
My-Right Hand-to-God
  Stanton
Noisy Stanton
Shirt Stanton
Skid Stanton
Slim Stanton
Weizo Stanton
Winslow Stanton
Craps Stipley
Legs Stipley
Petro Stipley
Big Tom Sullivan
Boy Sullivan
Corny Sullivan
Horseman Sullivan
Solo Sullivan
Big Sum Sweeney
Black Wings Sweeney
Blather Sweeney
Bunny Sweeney
Crooked Heels
  Sweeney
Gold Tooth Sweeney
Heeney Sweeney
Know-it-All Sweeney
Milky Mouth Sweeney
Mockie Sweeney
Moonglow Sweeney
Red Jim Sweeney
Red Muzzie Sweeney
Rock Sweeney
Short Shovel Sweeney

Sneaky Sweeney
Yank Sweeney

T

Pauper Taafe
Polly Taylor
Skinny Taylor
Crab Terrell
Boots Thomas
Shoo-Fly Thompson
Rusty Tierney
Chick Toms
Hopper Toolis
Mackeral Mouth Toolis
Ockie Toolis
Vestie Toolis
Socket Toomey
Itchie Traelis
Tish Trapnell
Dinny Trodden

V

Hammer Head Varner

W

Hawkshaw Wagner
Pig Ears Wainwright
Frog Walker
Hump Walker
Slouchy Walker

Snout Walker
Bud Walsh
Caesar Walsh
Deadman Walsh
Duke Walsh
Ebby Walsh
Hard Man Walsh
Hess Walsh
Sleeper Walsh
Woo Num Walsh
Darby Ward
Duke Ward
Don't-Do-Anything-
    Until-You-Hear-
    From-Me Warren
Banty Watson
Butch Webb
Ike Weir
Little Ike Weir
Weary Willie Weir
John, James & Owen
    Welch: The Three
    Gentlemen

Mickey-the-Jigger
    Welch
Pudgie Welch
Spiker Welch
Tadder Welch
Walloper Welch
Gee Whiz Whalen
Humming Bird Whalen
Jodie Whalen
Jud Whalen
Big Head White
Chubby White
Largy White
Whizzer White
Chimney Williams
Redhead Williams
Scotty Williams
Twittzle Wittenberg
Stumpy Woods

Z

Bowley Zalewski

Clothes Make the Boy-o

Shirttail Finnerty came by his nickname honestly. His shirtail usually hung out.

There was good reason for this untidy state of clothing.

Finnerty was a member of a typically big Irish family, and in such families clothes usually would be handed down from one child to the next with little or no thought given to size or fit. Make-do was the operative word.

The boy's mother would hold high a garment in the line of transfer and observe in a loud voice (no doubt to ward off argument and protest): "This is perfectly good. There's not a brack on it."

None of the children knew what a brack looked like so they couldn't dispute the statement. Bracks, unchallenged, stood out as one of the family's small mysteries.

Finnerty's older brother, unfortunately, was much older and bigger than his next in line. Consequently, the shirts that this hapless boy inherited invariably were too large to be tucked successfully under his pants and usually had a way of continually working loose and flapping loosely behind him, like the tail on a kite.

Shirttail was the word for Finnerty.

In the Line of Duty

Among the many highlight happenings during the annual St. Patrick's Day parades in Cleveland was one in which a prominent West Side doctor combined his professional talent with his obligatory display of Irish pride.

Among the marchers on that eventful day in 1970 was Dr. Thomas J. Barrett, an obstetrician, and he never was in better form as he swung proudly down Euclid Avenue, waving aloft his kelly-green forceps, especially dyed for the great day.

Thousands of spectators lined the parade route, to be sure, but Dr. Barrett's alert eye still spotted in the crowd one of his female patients, Peg O'Neill Cooney, as she stood at the curbside, enthusiastically cheering on the paraders.

Without breaking step, Dr. Barrett moved away from the main company of marchers and sidled toward his patient, whom he knew was already past the estimated day of delivery. Once he was within vocal range, he sternly ordered Mrs. Cooney to go home immediately, take to an easy chair, and put her feet up on a stool.

"Begone," shouted the doctor, waving the forceps for emphasis, "and not another word out of you!"

His duty done, Dr. Barrett sidestepped back into line and resumed his patriotic march.

(Mrs. Cooney did as she was ordered. A week later, on March 24th, she gave birth to a 10-pound newcomer named Brian O'Neill Cooney.)

A Little Goes a Long Way

One of the legendary characters in the old Angle was a man who was known as Little Liquor O'Neill.

All things considered, it isn't surprising that O'Neill, a soft-spoken and polite man, was a steady customer in the neighborhood bars where he regularly displayed a technique that would not be denied. It was his habit to perch wistfully on a stool with an empty glass in front of him on the bar, creating a picture of longing that tugged at the heartstrings of other patrons.

When the bartender or a generous customer would respond to that picture by offering to buy him a drink, O'Neill was always properly grateful in his acceptance, but with the nice restraint that always goes with good manners.

"Sure and I'll be glad to join you," he would say, "but just a little now, don't you know."

They say he averaged about 40 of the "little" drinks a day.

Who could deny him a nickname so honestly won?

The Miracle of Television

The American way of life never ceased to amaze a Mayo man who, like so many other immigrants from the Emerald Isle, took up a career in Cleveland as a member of the Cleveland Fire Department. Everything he saw in this strange new world tested his powers of acceptance. His voiced wonderment over even common artifacts like the automatic toaster was a continuing source of entertainment to the men of Hook & Ladder Company No. 12, which, at the time of this telling, was stationed in the firehouse on W. 114th Street, just off Detroit Avenue.

Let this highly likeable man be called Desmond; Desi for short. It was not his name, but it will do. He was a good fireman, mind you, and his devotion to duty took him, in time, to the distinguished level reserved for lieutenants. But if he took on an officer's badge and authority, Desi never lost his naivete concerning things American. He could never reconcile the ways of the Angle, say, with those of Achill Island, while the larger world beyond Cleveland's West Side left him completely mystified.

None of this escaped the attention of the other firemen of Hook & Ladder Company No. 12, to be sure, but Desi, in their view, reached his innocent peak on a memorable day in 1950. It was an incident that had nothing to do with blazing buildings or heroic rescues. It was the day that a television receiver was installed in the fire house.

That was an early time in the history of television, to be sure, and it didn't matter what was on the 10-inch screen, it was received by one and all as a miracle in being. The idea of pictures being transmitted through the air was nothing less than wondrous, and Desi was more impressed by the new medium than any of his comrades. In his eyes it was the greatest miracle since the division of the loaves and fishes on the shores of Galilee. He watched everything that appeared on the screen with rapt attention, to the extent that when the fire alarm rang, he had to be tugged loose of his chair in front of the TV set. And when the company returned from a fire, he would reclaim his vantage point without even taking off his boots.

One night, in the company of a fellow fireman, Francis J. McDonald, Desi gave his full attention to a program that arose on the screen, emitting a small cry of approval when the name of the show was announced. It was the Edgar Bergen & Charlie McCarthy program.

"Will you listen to that, now," he said to McDonald. "McCarthy is on this program. One of our own."

As the program unrolled, Desi gave it close study, but there was a look of puzzlement over what he was seeing and hearing, and when the program ended, he turned to McDonald and asked:

"Francis, what was wrong with that kid's legs?"

McDonald shook off his disbelief, but ever a witty man and always ready to go along with a joke, he replied, with a mock tone of regret in his voice: "I believe the kid had polio, Des."

Des shook his head indignantly. He was plainly offended.

"It's a crying shame," he cried. "They shouldn't ought to show a kid like that on television!"

Hitting the Bottle to Advantage

Bottles Brennan, like most in the neighborhood, was from a poor family; perhaps poorer than most. And, like most, he came by his nickname honestly.

Whenever the fellows wanted to go to a movie or visit the corner drug store for a soda, Bottles would ask them to wait a few minutes and then he would disappear.

Nobody could quite figure out how he did it, but, true to his promise, he would show up a few minutes later with a cluster of empty pop bottles under his arm. These he would take to a store and cash them in at a nickel apiece, thereby financing the trip to the movies or the guzzling of the fountain fizz.

The quest for El Dorado was nothing compared to the search of the neighborhood kids for the treasure of pop bottles they knew Brennan had hidden somewhere. But they never found it, and Brennan never revealed his secret trove.

With a Song on His Lips

The ranks of colorful people in Cleveland have thinned out shockingly since the glory days after World War II when Short Vincent Street, the downtown center of eccentricity, was host every night in the week to hundreds of characters who, by the very nature of their being, stood apart in an interesting way from the rest of society.

Everything about such individuals challenged understanding. They were different—and society, as we all know, has difficulty grappling with any departure from its own normal dullness. It eyes the odd man out with suspicion, if not active disapproval.

It is a telling truth, though, that people who refuse to follow a routine life frequently radiate a personality glow that attracts admirers as the flame draws the moth. It could be that the very differences that set them apart do, in fact, fuel their own personal flame and heighten the glow.

James F. O'Malley, jr., was just such a bright standout against the dull burlap background of the daily humdrum that passes for life with most people, even though he was conventional enough in his youth to follow in his father's path by working as a printer at the Plain Dealer. The senior James F. O'Malley, in fact, once had been president of the Printers Union.

The very fact that Junior elected to work as a printer by way of an adult sideline is itself a revelation of an individualistic leaning. Printers are artists, and most of them have the artist's craving for self expression. Print shops have attracted many uncommon characters through the years. Benjamin Franklin, for example, was neither ordinary nor conventional. Neither was a certain Plain Dealer printer who, in more recent times, served as the president of a nudist colony on the outskirts of Cleveland. (The outskirts, mind you, were suburbs, not clothes.)

As much as he liked a printer's life, the workaday world was no more than a minor distraction to Junior O'Malley, an unpretentious man who marched to the beat of his own drummer. The main route of that march led directly to the nearest race track, as it so often does with the horse-loving Irish. The Plain Dealer job undoubtedly interfered with O'Malley's vision of the world as it ought to be.

Everything about horse racing appealed to him: The natural competitiveness of the sport, the roar of the grandstand, the excitement of the bet, and, of course, the simple beauty of the sleek thoroughbreds as they stretched out in their basic rivalry on the track below. Except for his family and his religion, it was all that Junior O'Malley wanted out of life. But he was realistic enough to know that one day the fun would end, and while he took the overall prospect in stride, he did admit to friends that he was worried about one of the details of the ceremony attendant to his final departure.

"Who's going to sing at my funeral?" he would ask.

He tried to answer the question himself, back in the 1950s, when he wrung from Frank Gibbons, an outstanding sports columnist of the Cleveland Press, a promise that he would do the vocal honors at Junior's funeral. Gibbons had a fine singing voice which he let out of its cage every winter when he was called on to sing in the annual "Ribs 'n Roasts" musical revue featuring sportswriters. But Gibbons, alas, passed away at much too early a date, effectively cancelling out any future funeral performances in behalf of friends.

The frustrated O'Malley in time turned to his longtime friend, Danny Coughlin, the ubiquitous sportswriter-sportscaster, not for his singing talent, wisely, but for his advice. Coughlin's pipes would have put the chill on a reunion of the Addams family, as Junior well knew from ear-witness experiences in which the noted reporter had out bellowed the house in several saloon sing-alongs.

In his sad recital of the failures he had met in his search for a funeral singer, Junior revealed that he had come close to success one time when still another friend had agreed to be the vocalist after Frank Gibbons had passed away.

"He promised to do it," brooded O'Malley, "but then, wouldn't you know, he up and died too."

Word naturally got around, in time, that agreeing to sing at Junior's funeral was itself life-threatening. None of his friends, not even the worst singers, would even discuss the assignment, much less accept it. He was discouraged.

"I've got an idea," said Coughlin. "Why don't you do your own singing at the funeral?"

O'Malley gave him a pitying look.

"Sure," he said, "and wouldn't that be a neat trick!"

"Think about it," said Coughlin. "We could record you singing a song and we could play it back on the big day! I can hear it now. You singing 'Ave Maria,' say, and everybody in the church crying their eyes out."

"'Ave Maria?' interrupted O'Malley. "If I sang that, there's no doubt but that everybody would be in tears.

No, the tune I want somebody to sing is that old favorite, 'Ace in the Hole.'"

Coughlin blinked and paused to regroup.

"'Ace in the Hole'? Why not? I went to a wedding once where they played 'Raindrops Keep Falling on My Head,' pronounced 'Haid.' Music is music. What matters is that you're the right guy to sing at your own funeral. I mean it. You're a pretty good singer, I know, and you could belt out that song with a lot of feeling and sincerity. That's important, especially at a funeral."

O'Malley silently mulled over the idea. The more he thought about it, the more he liked it. The sands were running low and he had little time to make a really suitable arrangement. Coughlin's suggestion, furthermore, appealed to his broad sense of humor. After all, it was *his* funeral. Why shouldn't he sing?

"I'll do it," he said.

"Fine," said Coughlin, the master showman. "I'll make all the arrangements. Leave it to me."

Thus it came about one night shortly thereafter, as the patrons of Swingos' Silver Quill restaurant on the Lakewood Gold Coast were settling back in well-fed expectation of entertainment by the famous singing quartet, The Four Lads, Danny Coughlin appeared center stage and took the microphone.

Coughlin, a prominent radio and television personality, was quickly recognized by most of the diners, all of whom shared a certain wonderment, even fear, as to his role in the evening's entertainment program.

"Hello!" pondered one of the customers, thoughtfully patting his goatee with a napkin, "What do we have here? A sports bulletin perhaps?"

Coughlin quickly ended such speculation with his big announcement; namely, that the lucky customers were in for a special treat in the person of a guest vocalist, Junior O'Malley.

"Mr. O'Malley will sing that beloved old ballad, 'Ace in the Hole,'" Coughlin announced, his voice resonant with professional gravity. "The Four Lads will join in his rendition, which, by the way, will be recorded. Live, if you please. It is planned that the recording will be played back at Mr. O'Malley's funeral, which, we all trust, will be a long time in the distant future."

There was considerable stirring about among the customers. The situation had an awkward side. They didn't know whether to take the annoucement seriously, and if they did, whether they should applaud. Was applause appropriate? No matter what, they all sensed they were part of a Show Business first; history in the making.

Junior O'Malley stepped forward and relieved the puzzling situation with his usual aplomb and a nononsense beginning. He took the microphone from Coughlin, smiled at the audience, nodded to the Four Lads, and began to sing. He had a fine voice and it blended nicely with the harmonic background provided by the famous quartet. The result may have been the best rendition ever of "Ace in the Hole"; probably better than even the composer could have hoped for.

This much is beyond dispute. The ending was different. As the last note faded away, Junior addressed himself to eternity, saying:

"So long, everybody. I hope there's a race track up here!"

The diners, having gotten into the spirit of the occasion by that time, gave Junior an enthusiastic ovation. The applause was loud and prolonged, joined in by the musicians and the star quartet, and even some knife-and-fork thumping on the linen by a few of the customers. Any professional singer would have been grateful for the audience response.

When, some time later, it became clear that Junior O'Malley's time on earth was fast running out, Coughlin went to the pastor of St. Rose's Church on Detroit Avenue and W. 116th Street and confided in him the plan to play Junior's recording at the end of the funeral Mass. The astonished priest, not surprisingly, would have none of the plan. He thought a post-mortem solo improper.

It came about, though, that when Junior O'Malley's race against time crossed the finish line at the Holy Family Cancer Home, the pastor was away in Rome. The celebrant of the funeral Mass would be Auxiliary Bishop A. James Quinn, a lifelong friend of Junior.

Danny Coughlin, still carrying on in his friend's behalf, didn't have a chance to discuss all the finer points of the funeral mass with the bishop, but it didn't matter. It was a grand ceremony and in his homily the prelate had some lovely things to say about the deceased.

There also was a very nice touch at the end when Denise Dufala, a television news anchorwoman, sang "Ave Maria" in a professional performance. When she had finished, the pallbearers began to move the casket slowly down the aisle in the final recessional. It was the signal for Denise to push the "play" button of the recorder that Coughlin thoughtfully had put at her side. Immediately the church was filled with the sound of Junior O'Malley's voice, backed by the Four Lads, in the singing of *Ace in the Hole* (George Mitchell and James Dempsey, composers; Jerry Vogel Music Company, Inc., Publishers).

The startled mourners, many of them familiar with Junior's voice, twisted around and looked toward the choir loft in wonder. Bishop Quinn, no doubt as surprised as everyone else, discreetly stood with bowed head while Junior sang his heart out.

"This town is full of guys
Who think they're mighty wise
Just because they know a thing or two;
You can see them night and day
Strolling up and down Broadway,
Telling of the wonders they can do;
There's con men and boosters
And card sharps and crapshooters;
They congregate around the Metropole,
They wear fancy ties and collars,
And where they get their dollars,
They all have that ace down in the hole."

There was a pause after the song ended.

The big climax came with Junior's last spoken words:

"So long, everybody, I hope there's a race track up here."

Some of the people in the pews applauded, some dabbed at their eyes over the emotional climax, and some even smiled.

This much was certain: Junior, working against long odds, had come up with a classic of a funeral. He had finished far out in front of the field in his last outing, a magnificent run for the roses that were piled high in tributes from his friends and admirers.

Sergt. Muldoon at Valley Forge

The Irish gift for creativity and improvisation is admirably illustrated in one of the experiences of former Cleveland mayor, Thomas A. Burke, jr., having to do with his need to make a St. Patrick's Day speech at a banquet. The affairs of state weighed heavily on the city's chief executive at the time and he turned to his executive secretary, John Patrick Butler, for some material which he might incorporate in his speech.

Butler shrewdly passed the assignment along to a talented young Cleveland radio writer, Thomas O'Connell, who never allowed humdrum facts to interfere with any of his literary dramas. He responded with a speech so dramatic that the mayor himself choked with emotion as he delivered it at the civic banquet.

The script recalled the role of the Irish volunteers in the Revolutionazry War and stressed, in particular, their suffering and heroism in the terrible fighting at Valley Forge. Singled out for special commendation was a Sergt. Muldoon, who was likened favorably by the mayor to Audie Murphy, the outstanding combat hero of World War II.

After the speech, which drew loud cheers and much thumping of knives and forks on the banquet tables, Mayor Burke, flushed with satisfaction, turned to his father, Dr. Thomas A. Burke, who had sat impassively at his side throughout the talk.

"What did you think of the speech, Dad?" asked the mayor.

"It was fine, son," said Dr. Burke, "and your delivery was excellent."

"Thank you," said the mayor. "It seemed to me, though, that you listened with a certain reservation, as if there were points with which you could not agree."

"That's true," his father said, nodding his head. "You are perceptive. There were a few minor points that I had to question. You see, Tom, Valley Forge was nothing more than a winter encampment. There was no fighting there for Sergt. Muldoon or anyone else except the fight to survive the winter.

"Another thing, Tom, I've made a study of the Revolutionary War, and I can tell you there was nobody by the name of Sergt. Muldoon in Washington's army.

"Other than that, it was a fine story you told and one that was most appropriate to the occasion, even if it was inaccurate. You should compliment your Mr. O'Connell on his imagination and his gift for creative writing."

Mulraney and the Milkman

It is indisputably true that there are certain characteristics common to the Irish. A lot of them sing tenor. Some of them have quick tempers. Many of them have the gift of gab. A large number of them have been known to have an inordinate craving for the creature. Most of them have a deep affection for horses. And who would deny their love of a good fight?

You mix all of these traits together and, searching for an example embodying all of the characteristics, you come to the recollection of a certain Irishman-about-town who, out of sheer timidity, we shall give the name of Mulraney.

Mulraney was a rotund man whose physique once was favorably compared with the back of a city bus. He was a brave and willing fire fighter who never shirked his duty and whose record of performance during his many years on the department was unblemished.

On the other hand his record, off-duty, was something else. It seems he not only was a willing drinker, but one who was always on the ready with his fists. Smart barroom regulars were quick to sense as much and Mulraney had few challengers during his drinking hours.

In the early hours of a particular morning when Mulraney was making his way home in a depressed mood, having been unable to find a single challenger in his favorite pub, he came upon a milkman who was going from house-to-house, innocently dropping off odd bottles of milk along the route—with help, to be sure, from his horse and wagon.

Arguments begin in many different ways that often are hard to trace. It wasn't that way with the argument that sprang up between Mulraney and the milkman. Mulraney always played the role of provocateur. Much to the milkman's surprise, no doubt, the two men squared off. It was probably the first time in the long nighttime that Mulraney was happy. The two men exchanged blows, but not in equal number. Mulraney had much the better of the unfair exchange and the milkman, sensibly realizing that he was on the short end, ran off into the dawn mists, leaving behind him Mulraney, the horse, and the milk wagon.

Mulraney's mood quickly changed from the joy brought on by combat to anger over the milkman's forfeiture and withdrawal. He looked about him in fury, tore a slat off a picket fence, and whacked the poor gelding on the rump.

"You son of a bitch!" he yelled at the startled horse, "you were with him!"

And that happened years before anyone thought of guilt by association.

Hark! the Herald's a Boy

Harky Herald was the member of a large family which, until his arrival, consisted only of girls.

The elder Herald was more than pleased to be the father of a bouncing baby boy and grew outright rhapsodic as he proclaimed to one and all that the new child was nothing less than a gift from the angels.

That reminded somebody of the carol, *Hark the Herald Angels Sing,* and in no time at all the lad had a name for life: Harky Herald.

Dominus Vobiscum

John Patrick Butler, one of the leading figures in governmental and legal circles in modern times, is the subject of many stories that enliven any gathering of judges and lawyers.

Butler long has been acknowledged as one of the truly brilliant attorneys through his many triumphs in cases involving the criminal law, but in his wake he also has left a lot of his colleagues in a state of confusion and uncertainty because his sense of humor so often tested the limits of credibility.

The courtroom crowd in Cleveland still talk about the time one of their own, a lawyer known for his intellectual limitations as well as his gullibility, approached Butler and asked for help in a particularly difficult case centered on domestic troubles.

Butler listened to the circumstances gravely and nodded his understanding as he clapped a hand on the fellow-lawyer's shoulder and assured him he had in mind just the solution to his problem.

"The judge hearing your case," he said shrewdly, "is Irish, I believe."

"That is true," said the lawyer, already impressed.

"Very well," said Butler, "when you are in court tomorrow, I want you to stand up, at the first opening, and tell the judge you would like to file a motion of Dominus Vobiscum."

"What's that?" said the lawyer, puzzled. "Irish talk?"

"No," said Butler, "that's Latin.'

The lawyer was impressed.

"It sounds good," he said, "but what does it mean?"

Butler shook his head patiently.

"It means just what it says," he said.

"Maybe so," said the lawyer, "but will the judge understand Latin?"

"Of course," roared Butler. "Why do you think they made him a judge?"

"That's true," acknowledged the lawyer apologetically.

The next day in court the lawyer followed Butler's suggestion and got an immediate result. That is to say, he brought the trial to a standstill. The baffled prosecutor sent one of his assistants scurrying to the law library to find out what this fancy motion meant. The judge, to his credit, merely bobbed his head and declared a brief recess, allowing him to regain his judicial composure in the privacy of his chambers.

Not only did the judge understand Latin, he also understood that the fine non-italian hand of John Patrick Butler was involved in this unprecedented motion. The criminal lawyer's elliptical sense of humor was well known to the judiciary.

At any rate, things worked out nicely for all concerned. The lawyer who made the motion gained new stature in the eyes of his colleagues for his casual use of a dead language. More important, the defendant whom he represented came out the winner.

Even Butler gained fresh prestige as the lawyer whom he had helped spread the word around the courthouse that Butler had been a a big help to him in the case. And from that day on, wherever he went, even at cocktail parties, the lawyer liked to let those fateful words roll off his tongue: Dominus Vobiscum!

The Power of Speech

Thomas (Bumpy) Kilbane was the business agent of Local 310 of the Laborers and Hodcarriers Union, and his talent for saying a lot in a few words undoubtedly helped to win him that influential office.

Kilbane's knack for positive thinking was best demonstrated when he allowed that Hitler and Mussolini were "the two greatest business agents that ever lived."

"They put everybody to work but Donuts Gallagher and Louis (The Dip) Finkelstein," observed Kilbane.

Donuts Had a Word for It

The friends and associates of a popular West Sider named John (Donuts) Gallagher respected him for many things, his command of the English language among them. One of his admirers described Gallagher's vocabulary as "running the gamut from light crystal to deep purple."

Donuts was a confirmed bachelor, a voracious reader, and had the ability to make the language work for him, often in an elliptical way. His old world type of courtesy was especially marked when he addressed women. On one occasion when he was introduced to a pretty girl, he bowed and told her that while she was charming, she was "not quite as pretty as her mother."

It goes without saying that he liked to eat doughnuts. From such a simple craving do nicknames sometimes spring.

The Parade That Almost Wasn't

Weather, as a rule, never was seen as a determining factor in the annual celebration of St. Patrick's Day in Cleveland except as a minor source of discomfort and possibly as an excuse for staying close to a warm barroom. There was one historic year, however, when the elements exceeded their own intemperate limits and turned loose on the town one of the worst blizzards in its history.

The day was so bad, would you believe it, that the planners of the parade were persuaded to postpone the grand march up and down the streets of Cleveland?

The news was not well received in all quarters. There were some Hibernians sensitive to world opinion who felt that any refusal to march simply because of a howling blizzard would be taken by outsiders as an unmistakable sign that the Irish were on the decline, if they had not already succumbed to the easy-going ways of a decadent society.

A few stout celebrators representing the legal profession came together in outraged concern when they heard the terrible news. After debating the courses of action open to them including a few caveats, some mandamuses, and even an outright habeas corpus, they agreed on a simple plan calculated to embarrass the timid parade leaders. They would, at personal risk, stage their own march through the streets in a public demonstration of Celtic hardiness.

"The mail carriers won't be stopped by the weather and neither will we!" roared a spokesman. "The honor of the Irish is at stake."

Somewhere these protestors found an Irish flag, an American flag, two bagpipers who considered bagpiping more important than freezing to death, and 13 like-minded stalwarts who were so embarrassed by all the amateurs crowding the rail at Pat Joyce's Bar on Chester Avenue and Manus McCaffery's place in the old Hollenden Hotel that they felt it their bounden duty to defy the elements.

"Sure, there's more to St. Patrick's Day than just drinking!" cried out one of the lawyers, drawing startled looks from all sides of him at the bar.

It was no more than a corporal's guard at best that took to the streets, but that doughty band of officers of the court bravely went out into the driving snow and marched as promised, carefully following the official route through the downtown that had been laid out for the big parade. Unfortunately, thanks to the blizzard, there were no curbside spectators, but a number of parade fanciers looking on from behind office windows along the route pronounced the procession a decided success if only for its unusual demonstration of barrister brotherhood.

There was general agreement from the same onlookers that even though the March of the Legal Lights was virtually private in nature, it was terribly symbolic of something or other, and from that standpoint very much worthwhile even if it afterward took an extraordinary quantity of Irish whiskey to thaw out the marchers.

The bagpipers especially needed special ministration because their lips had gotten frozen in a kind of permanent pucker, and one of them, months later, was still complaining that his knees still hadn't thawed out completely and that his wife was very unhappy about that.

The most important effect of the extraordinary substitute parade on that historic day was the guilt felt by the people who had failed to take their place along the curbside. It wouldn't have been surprising if the heroic lawyers had sued them for lack of support.

Freckles & His Friends

Freckles are not uncommon among the Irish, but it was said that Strawberry Dunn had the world's biggest and best freckles. Not only were they large, they were mottled and shaped like ripe strawberries, a distinction that set him apart and above the everyday crowd of Irish freckle-faces.

The Cowboy at Large

Long before James Thurber brought Walter Mitty and his world of fantasies onto the literary scene, there was a likeable West Side Irishman named Cornelius (Cowboy) Lee who was entirely familiar with the make-believe areas of the mind. One of his long-time friends and associates observed that Cowboy never got bored on a job because "he never was really there."

"He was always off in Fantasy Land," he said. "He was there long before Walt Disney thought of the place."

The Cowboy, a steamfitter by trade, worked for the Standard Brewing company for many years. Once, in the performance of his duties, he was dispatched to a bar in Lakewood in answer to a complaint from the proprietor that the Standard beer delivered to his saloon was flat.

Lee walked silently into the bar, unannounced, and while the bartender-owner looked on with deep interest, he went behind the bar and poured a sample draught from the keg into a stein. Then, smacking his lips and rolling his eyes appreciatively upward, he announced in a loud voice to one and all that the beer he had just personally tasted was alive and well; certainly not flat as alleged by some inexpert bartenders.

The owner of the saloon nodded his head in agreement.

"The only trouble is," he pointed out to the Cowboy, "the beer you just drank came from a Carling's keg. The Standard beer is on the other side of the cash register, and it's flat as hell!"

The Case of the Sleepy Bailiff

Among Cleveland's many interesting people in the early decades of the century was a pixiesh court bailiff named Francis (Pick) Mulhall. The origin of his interesting nickname stirred a lot of speculation. Some of his friends thought it to be an abbreviation of "picturesque" because, by all accounts, he was that. The real story behind the name, however, was that he was the youngest child in a very large Irish family, and at a very early age he was identified as "the pick of the litter." In such a sensible way are nicknames born.

Court bailiffs, it should be explained, seldom lead exciting lives. Sometimes a trial of a sensational nature comes along and stirs their interest, but the daily routine usually is taken by nasty crimes committed by nasty people and the cumulative effect can be downright torporous.

One day as a trial droned on in the courtroom of Municipal Judge Hugh Corrigan, Pick dozed off in spite of himself and was having a refreshing nap until the defense lawyer, an inconsiderate type at best, raised his voice several notches above normal. They say he was encouraged to yell because one of the jurors kept cupping his right ear, a terribly provocative gesture in the sight of any lawyer.

Whether the lawyer's outburst succeeded in getting through to the hearing-impaired juror is not known, but it did wake up Pick Mulhall. He, startled into consciousness and thinking the trial was just about to get underway, jumped to his feet and made the traditional outcry opening a court session;

"Hear ye! Hear ye! . . . "

Nobody was more taken aback by this loud and untimely interruption than His Honor, who then had to placate the ruffled lawyer and restore order in the confused courtroom. He was an expert gaveler, fortunately, and subdued the room quickly.

Judge Corrigan, mind you, not only was a longtime friend of Pick's, he also was a most understanding man. There were many times, he knew, when he himself was tempted to doze off during a court hearing. In this instance, he simply gave the abashed bailiff a disapproving nod of the head and what might be called a suspended sentence. But he did strike back in his own mischievous way.

Not long after the "Hear ye, Hear ye" incident, a prostitute with a long record of arrests, appeared in Corrigan's court, but the circumstances were such that he placed her on probation. When she came to thank him afterward, the judge told her that the person she ought to thank was Pick Mulhall for intervening in her behalf.

Mulhall, a bachelor who was downright skittish in the presence of women, had done no such thing, and when the woman started tracking him down through the corridors of City Hall, determined to thank him, he took to his heels, darting in and out of hiding places whenever she came near until she finally wearied of the chase.

In the meantime, everybody in City Hall, including the judge, enjoyed Pick's discomfiture. He never again fell asleep during a trial.

The Road to Ruane

A Clevelander, Terry Joyce, on a sentimental journey back to County Mayo, the place of his birth, was having difficulty finding a friend's house in Ballynrobe when, fortuitously, he met a pipe-smoking postman riding a bicycle along the road.

"Pardon me," said Joyce, "but could you tell me if I'm on the right road to the homestead of Myles Ruane?"

The mailman took the pipe from his mouth, tapped it against the palm of his hand, and offered a deliberate reply.

"My dear man," he said kindly, "if you were on any other road, you would be on the wrong one."

The Battler from Linndale

The most curious community by far in the metropolitan complex known as Greater Cleveland is a place called Linndale.

It is officially listed as a suburb, but that is sheer flattery. To call it a community is overreaching. To describe it as a town or village would be exaggeration. Only a generous onlooker would dignify it as anything more than a large neighborhood.

Linndale, in any category, still would have on its side the kind of history that only a humorless world would choose to brush aside.

This is a very old, very small, enclave that can trace its existence back to the very wilderness days of Brooklyn, the original West Side township that took in all the territory on the sunset side of the Cuyahoga Valley. It languished on the outskirts of Cleveland in the general vicinity of W. 117th Street (Highland Avenue) and Bellaire Avenue, as an agreeable patch of country with a nice setting of trees and meadows until the middle of the 19th century. When the railroad appeared on the pastoral scene at that time, conditions changed.

The Big Four Railroad, one of the intruders, chose to build its roundhouse and a small passenger station in Linndale, and those rail facilities became the civic core of the tiny town. Such population as would own up to residential status in the flush years leading to World War II consisted mainly of railroad workers and their families.

That was the way things stood for a century or so, until the roundhouse and passenger station closed down in the sorry postwar years of railroading. It was thought then by experts in such matters that Linndale, like the old tracks, would finally rust in peace.

It was not to be so. Peace, in the sense of civic tranquility, never has been a noticeable characteristic of Linndale life either in the past or the present. Controversy has marked its long history and still persists in the embattled village. Generational changes in this community have had no mellowing effect on its bellicose personality. It continues to be the closest thing to an independent fiefdom as it goes on its traditional path, a questionable line that narrowly separates the law from the outlaw.

Tiny as the town is with its population somewhere less than 100 souls, there was a time some 70 years ago when the name of Linndale was known from coast to coast and beyond simply because it was the home ground, the bailiwick, of Battling Tom O'Malia.

O'Malia, a tall, lean man with admirable biceps, served two terms as the elected mayor of Linndale beginning in 1928. Prior to that time, he had served as the town marshal. He filled the role to perfection. Wyatt Earp never enjoyed such success in office. When Tom O'Malia buckled his belt and walked out onto the street, it was High Noon. The bad guys scattered. So did the good guys. The marshal didn't discriminate when it came to choosing his targets.

Battling Tom once was described in a news story as "lanky and pugnacious." It was no understatement. He was six feet tall and he had been a prize fighter in his early years, but that arena of combat was not to his liking. It was too confining. O'Malia fared better outside the ring where he was not fettered by the kind of sissy rules handed down by the likes of the effete Marquis of Queensbury.

O'Malia first arrested national attention after his election to the town marshal's post in 1927. Linndale, being beyond the reach of Cleveland authorities, played host to all kinds of questionable elements during the Prohibition years. Bootleg establishments, usually private clubs with peepholes in the doors, flourished in the vicinity of Memphis and Bellaire Avenues, the main streets of the town.

Marshal O'Malia wasn't a reformer. He enjoyed the Wild West atmosphere that prevailed as much as any of the patrons who flocked into the town from across the line. He was a realist and he knew that the illegal joints gave Linndale the financial support it needed. A story in the *Cleveland News* at the time of his death in 1939 recalled his brief career as a law enforcement officer.

"The marshal not only swore out warrants against residents whom he accused of violating laws, but had many charges placed against him by irate citizens.

"Charges of robbery, blackmail and malicious destruction of property, placed against him following a liquor raid in 1928, were dismissed when the prosecuting witness failed to appear for a hearing."

It wasn't until his election as mayor in 1928 that O'Malia began to realize his full potential as a national newsmaker. He did that mainly with his fists. Sometimes it would be the bad guys that he pounded, but he was just as likely to make a point with his fists in the hall of village government.

Reporters from the Cleveland newspapers looked forward to the Monday night meetings of the Linndale town council because they were such productive breeding grounds for entertaining news, thanks to the mayor.

The Associated Press and United Press wires made merry from coast to coast with their stories of Mayor O'Malia punching out a disagreeable councilman or a town patrolman.

At one time during the Prohibition years, the official census count in Linndale claimed 381 citizens in residence, raising a considerable outcry from onlooking skeptics who charged that the figure was padded. It didn't matter really because shortly thereafter a new highway called the Medina Freeway pierced the heart of the settlement and eliminated 48 of the existing 99 houses.

Linndale, on the positive side, not only provided a happy refuge to people who sought to challenge the temperance law, it also gave cover to otherwise homeless gamblers and the outlawed purveyors of fireworks. The presence of the fireworks stands on Bellaire and Memphis Avenues used to infuriate proper Clevelanders striving to promote a Safe and Sound Fourth.

On the other hand, there were many more citizens who privately felt a little stirring of pride in the way the spunky little town defied all the rules and conventions of the day. In Mayor O'Malia they saw the personification of resistance to the nameless, shapeless uniformity that began to characterize the rest of the country at the beginning of the 20th Century. Whatever the reason, millions of Americans chuckled every time they read another wire service story about that strange mayor in the Cleveland area who had just broken up another council meeting with his fists. He did stand in refreshing contrast to all the pompous, stuffy, proper, dull, holier-than-thou politicians who held control almost everywhere outside of Linndale.

Linndale was not entirely alone in its peculiar politics. The town of Newburyport, Massachusetts, at the time had its Battling Tom counterpart in its mayor, best known as Bossy Gillis. O'Malia and Gillis were a matching pair. Gillis, like O'Malia, was a pugnacious Irishmen, and, like O'Malia, his unorthodox conduct often was outside the political pale.

The Linndale mayor, with some resentment, saw the Newburyport mayor as a copycat competitor and challenged him to an open debate, or, if he preferred, to an open fistfight. O'Malia believed in being fair. Mayor Gillis, however, wisely chose to overlook the laying down of the gauntlet by the Ohioan.

"I can hit hard and shoot straight," O'Malia once told reporters when they inquired into his philosophy. "I like a good, clean fight, but I am strong for nice, clean, peaceful living."

O'Malia could have added that he also was strong for freedom. He endorsed it many times while in office and exemplified it in his conduct, claiming the freedom especially to punch out anybody who opposed him.

There actually was more freedom for individual Americans in Linndale on the 4th of July than could be found anywhere else in Ohio, or, for that matter, in the contiguous 48 states. Linndale citizens and their friends were free to buy booze, free to gamble, and free to shoot skyrockets upward, willy nilly, as they chose on that national holiday while other millions of Americans had to celebrate with lemonade, a furious game of checkers, or lighting some illicit sparklers.

It wasn't that Mayor O'Malia believed in outright anarchy. He knew when to draw the line, as he did in one of his most highly publicized cases. That was the time he threatened to jail a Linndale citizen unless he kept his hog from wallowing in one of the village's dirt streets.

Interestingly enough, Marshal O'Malia himself was arrested by his political enemies almost as many times as he arrested them. It was not entirely a one-sided relationship.

Battling Tom believed in law and order, not as defined in the books, but according to his own lights. A journalist of his time wrote: "It was a dull day during his (O'Malia's) four years in office if somebody wasn't circulating ouster petitions. If the boys got rowdy at the pool room, Fighting Tom went out bare-handed and brought 'em in alive—if not in perfect condition."

O'Malia did have the knack of confounding his opponents at critical times in his career. Once, when it seemed that ouster proceedings against him would succeed in driving him from the office of town marshal, he ran for mayor and was elected. In his victory speech he blithely told his critics they could take the marshal's shiny badge and, in effect, shove it. That did not go over too well with his enemies, but his admirers, especially the journalists of the day, loved it.

O'Malia, incidentally, won that mayoral election by 52 votes and he made a big point of telling the world that he personally had driven every one of those 52 voters to the polls. He believed in public service.

The pugnacious politician was a Cleveland native, born on the south Side to Irish immigrant parents. He showed marked promise as a baseball player in his youth and was signed to a Cleveland Indians contract. He was farmed out as a pitcher to the Los Angeles team in the Pacific Coast League for several years, but, failing to make the major league grade, he returned to Cleveland to try his hand at professional boxing. No doubt hampered by the ring rules, he turned to a job as a jewelry salesman before he settled down in the field for which he obviously was best qualified: politics.

Mayor O'Malia's most serious administrative concern during his two terms in officer was financial. It wasn't too severe a problem during Prohibition days when the gamblers and bootleggers were chipping in contributions to the village coffers, but deficit operation was a chronic condition nevertheless. O'Malia met one financial crisis head-on by selling part of the village to the Big Four Railroad, but that was an approach which, carried to the ultimate, offered little promise to the Linndale future.

The village under his direction ultimately turned to a not-so-original system of civic financing based on revenue from traffic tickets.

"The trouble is," O'Malia once openly complained, "the village is too small. The automobiles are in and out again before a person could catch them."

His solution to the problem was to have the council authorize boulevard stops where none logically would be expected by an innocent motorist. Those strangely located stop signs eventually were augmented by traffic lights and what authorities like to call "strict enforcement" as carried out by a begoggled motorcycle cop—the mayor himself.

O'Malia's master plan combining law and order on the village streets with Linndale's financial requirements established a village tradition that lived on far beyond his administration. Forty years later, the Medina Freeway was replaced by interstate highway, I-71, and since 440 yards of the new highway ran within the village's borders, the village chieftains invoked the O'Malia tradition by imposing law and order on that tiny section.

There were loud protests from motorists who pointed out that there was not even a direct connection between I-71 and Linndale, but the village government dismissed that argument as a mere technicality. They insisted it was their civic duty to curb the mad behavior of motorists speeding through Linndale's 440 yards of highway, and toward that end the village's three cops took turns hiding in the shadows of the Memphis Road overpass and nabbing motorist offenders running amok on I-71. The tactic was so successful that the village treasury realized up to $400,000 a year in fines levied by the Linndale mayor's court.

Mayor O'Malia would have been gratified by his old village's resourcefulness later in carrying on his system of financing civic expenses through strict law enforcement. There is no telling what heights Linndale would have reached in Battling Tom's day if he had had a busy interstate highway to target for law enforcement. The Big Four Railroad likely would have run through the village on golden tracks.

There can't be any denial of O'Malia's contributon to the long existing pattern of unorthodox behavior in the highest governmental levels of Linndale. One successor in the village's top office was so markedly individualistic that he was sent to jail in the mid-1980s when found guilty on bribry and gambling charges. That same mayor, Armand Masten, earlier had distinguished himself by reaching across a table to twist a councilman's nose. Nose-twisting, remember, is always a crowd pleaser with voters.

Previous to that incident, the arrest of a Linndale mayor for hijacking a liquor truck drew prolonged cheers and loud chortles from the steady drinkers in the village's many taverns; the same ones who voted for the female council member with an explosive right cross. During one council meeting she took offense at a male colleague's suggestion that her language was not ladylike and hit him with a punch that buckled his knees and gave him a new respect for women's rights.

Battling Tom O'Malia would have appreciated the steady course followed by his old home town as confirmation of his own policy of handling civic problems with gloves on.

Boxing gloves, that is.

Down to Earth Wisdom

They tell this story about Mike McLaughlin, a generous and gregarious West Side Irishman who made frequent trips to the land of his fathers through the years, and who never returned home without a few accounts of some unusual experiences.

One of his anecdotes had to do with the time he was riding down a rutted road in a rented jaunting cart when it suddenly veered to one side and rolled into a farm field before he could bring it to a halt.

Fortunately for McLaughlin, there was help at hand; a farmer and his two sons who were at work in the field. They came to his side immediately and put the cart back on the road where it belonged.

Mike, understandably, was grateful and showed his feeling by insisting that his three rescuers join him in a pub down the road for a round of drinks. It was the least he could do, he argued, and his new-found friends agreed that it would be impolite for them to refuse him.

As the day in the pub wore on, taking on a mellow glow, one of the farmer's sons turned to his father and pointed out the obvious.

"Dad," he said, "we've been here too long. There's still a lot of work to be done in the field, you know."

The father nodded his recognition of the obvious truth, and then showed why it is that older people so often get credit for being wise.

"Paddy," he said to the son, "when we get up in the morning, that field will still be there." Then, pointing to McLaughlin, he added: "But this American gentleman won't."

Skid Strikes Back

When scholars from the outside world try to make a deep analysis of a nickname and the person to whom it is attached, they face certain frustration. Some things in life simply arise out of simple circumstance and should not be subjected to examination by the deep thinkers. Nicknames would be an example.

Take the case of Skid Stanton.

When Martin J. Stanton was a young man in the early years of the century, he acquitted himself remarkably well on the dance floor. He was especially adept in executing a popular dance that required its performers to slip and slide along the floor, not unlike the tango. Not surprisingly, the dance was best known as The Skid Along, or, more commonly, as The Skid.

The price that Stanton paid for his mastery of that dance form was to find himself called "Skid" by friends and admirers. It was their way of paying tribute to his terpsichorean skill, but Stanton's sisters took an active dislike to the nickname and urged him to reject its use. But he wisely took the name philosophically. There isn't much that one can do under such circumstances, and, as he pointed out, "There are a lot worse things people could call me."

He was right, of course. For the rest of his life, this popular West Sider, a city fireman, was known as Skid Stanton.

It shouldn't be surprising that Stanton wore his nickname with philosophical disregard. By the very nature of his job, often perilous, a firefighter must learn to live evenly with moments of terror, interim periods of boredom, and the nuisance of bureaucratic rules. A firefighter has time in the lonely hours at the firehouse to ponder the verities and to study the passing parade called mankind.

There is a lot to be said for pondering, to be sure, but sometimes it may become a problem in itself, as it did at Cleveland's firehouses some years ago. It seems that too many firemen with nothing better to do as they awaited the clanging of the alarm bell enjoyed sitting outside their stations in the open air, openly inhaling and otherwise idly admiring the neighborhood street action.

The sight of the firemen in relaxed posture made a lot of taxpayers nervous and even, some instances, downright envious. There were indignant letters to the newspapers demanding to know why the firemen weren't out fighting fires and grumbling about the expense of supporting public employees who had nothing better to do than to sit outside the firehouse chewing on toothpicks and ogling pretty girls.

Such complaints in time rose through the literate echelon of public officials until they reached Higher Authorities, a nervous group at best. In quick reaction, the Chief of the Cleveland Fire Department, prodded by City Hall, issued a sternly worded directive forbidding firemen from sitting outside their fire stations between 7 a.m. and 7 p.m. The 12 hours so bracketed were significant, being the peak daylight hours for observant pedestrian and vehicular traffic moving past the firehouses.

In this departmental order, the chief, in Solomon-like wisdom, had run his fire axe down the middle of the 24-hour day; ruling, in effect, that his doughty followers could do as much outside lolling as they wished during the low-traffic hours when they would be either completely hidden in the dark or partly shrouded by the dusk. In either instance they would be effectively screened from the beady eyes of passing taxpayers.

The anti-lolling rule was honored more in the breech than in the observance. Firemen are independent spirits and there were many nice days when some of them elected to ignore the chief's injunction against outdoor sitting. It was on such a day, indeed, that two of their number, Congo Ryan and Skid Stanton, chose to flaunt the rule by sitting illegally and boldly in broad daylight in front of Station No. 23 at W. 85th Street and Madison Avenue.

They did not escape the attention of a motorist who had been halted by a traffic light at that intersection and who chose to address them in the bitter voice that taxpayers always reserve for people on the public payroll whom they consider malingerers.

"Pretty soft!" quoth the motorist. "Pretty soft!"

Skid Stanton promptly jumped to his feet and looked directly and menacingly at the critic. As he reached down and picked up the folding-type wooden chair on which he had been sitting, the motorist shifted gears, obviously ready to flee the scene and the wrath of the aroused firefighter. But he didn't know the soft-mannered Stanton.

"Hey, pal," said Skid to the critic, "if you think that sitting on a poor excuse of a chair like this is easy, you ought to try it sometime!"

The motorist shook his head and drove on as Congo and Skid resumed their seats and their meditative postures. The world of Madison Avenue kept on turning, meanwhile, just as if nothing at all had happened.

If the fire chief ever learned of their sitting violation, he never let on.